Kindergarten Kapers

Thirteen Units of Study for Early Childhood

By

Paulette Berry
Ruth Chapman
Deborah Harris
Ruth Marek
Esther Read

Publishers

T. S. DENISON & COMPANY, INC.
Minneapolis

T. S. DENISON & COMPANY, INC.

All rights reserved, including the right to reproduce this book, or portions thereof, except that permission is hereby granted to the purchaser to reproduce the materials contained herein, for instructional purposes, provided that such materials are not resold or distributed outside the purchaser's own area of instruction.

Printed in the United States of America

Standard Book Number: 513-01449-7
Copyright © 1976 by T. S. Denison & Co., Inc.
Minneapolis, Minn. 55431

CONTENTS

	PAGE
Self Image	7
COMMUNITY HELPERS	
Grocer	13
Postman	17
Fireman	21
Milkman	26
Policeman	29
Baker	32
Thanksgiving Unit	36
A Christmas Unit	42
Health	48
HOLIDAY UNIT	
Halloween	52
Abraham Lincoln	55
St. Patrick's Day	58
Easter	60
SEASONS	
Exploring Spring	68
Circus and Zoo Unit	71
Transportation	78
Farm Unit	93
Seashore Unit	101
Miscellaneous	104

SELF IMAGE

We're Different

POEMS

Some of us are tall and thin.
Several chubby have been.

One of you has hair so black,
And you wear it down your back.

Now take Mary's smile so nice.
Look her over once or twice.

All of us are not the same.
And from different families came.

To this school we all were sent.
And are glad we're different.

James and His Turtle

The turtle belongs to James.
Together they play some games.

One's usually hide and seek.
For his turtle is quite meek.

He hides his head and legs and tail.
James tries it too, but to no avail.

He finally decided to let things be.
Let turtles be turtles and me
Just be me!

ART

Make a chart of the five senses. Provide a sheet of paper on which are written the following statements: I have **2** eyes for seeing; I have **2** ears to hear with; I have **1** nose to smell with; I have **1** mouth to taste with; I have **2** hands to feel with. Leave space after each statement for children to paste appropriate pictures to explain statement. Example: For I have **2** eyes for seeing, the child may paste **2** pictures of things which he can see.

Draw a self portrait: Tell the child to draw a picture of the way he likes himself.

Make a chart of **Things I can Do:** The chart will list the children's names. When the child achieves a desired goal, he will place a picture representing that goal on his chart. When the child can see his accomplishments he feels great satisfaction. Sample chart follows on the next page.

SELF IMAGE
Things I Can Do chart

SELF IMAGE

This is Me

FINGERPLAY

This is me, and this is you.
(hold up pointer finger on right and
   left hands)
And these are all our friends.
(hold up all fingers)
Spread us out; this you can do.
Watch this one as he bends.

Some of us are tall and thin.
(make motion with hands)
Some of us are shorter.
One of us might have a twin.
One might have a brother.

Now bring us all together.
(hold fingers up)
Just see how nice we stand.
Oh, we'll be friends forever!
Like fingers on a hand.

Me

ACTION POEM

Look in the mirror
Who do you see?
It's someone special
Look, it's me!

Note: For a follow up, pass around a hand mirror and let each child look at himself. Point out something special about each child and let them talk among themselves about something different or special about each other. After each child has had a chance to look and talk, let the children draw pictures of themselves. The teacher may wish to show these and let the class guess who it is.

SELF IMAGE

A Special Person
(tune — "The Farmer in the Dell")

MUSIC

I am a special person.
A very special person.
I am a special person.
And I shall tell you why.

I have two hands to feel with.
I have two eyes to see with.
I have two ears to hear with.
And that is why.

I am a special person.
A very special person.
I am a special person.
And I shall tell you why.

I have a nose to smell with.
I have a mouth to taste with.
I am a special person.
And that is why.

STORY

Good for Something

"Why can't I look like Debbie?" Linda asked her teacher one Monday morning.

Miss Wood answered, "Why do you want to look like Debbie, Linda?"

"Because everyone likes her. Everyone says that her hair is pretty."

The children were sitting at the circle ready to tell what they had done over the weekend when Linda asked her question. Miss Wood wanted to understand what she felt.

Now all the children in the class looked toward Debbie. She sat on the floor with her legs folded under her. She smiled in a friendly manner when the children turned to look at her.

Miss Wood looked at Debbie as she spoke. "Yes, everyone likes Debbie. That is true. Her hair is pretty but do you notice what a nice smile she has? That is one of the reasons everyone likes her too."

Then Miss Wood turned to look at Linda. "Now Linda, I am going to tell you about you. Did you know that the students in this class like you too? Did you know that you have a beautiful voice? Did you know that when we go to the music room that many children try to listen to you sing because you sing so pretty?"

Miss Wood began speaking to all her students. "We are all different one from another but there are nice things about each

SELF IMAGE

one of us. Some of us are taller than others. Some of us have black hair. Some of us have brown hair and some are blond."

"Don't forget Susan's red hair!" Billy said.

"That's right," Miss Wood answered. "Susan has beautiful red curly hair."

"Also," Miss Wood continued, "all of us have different talents. Some of us can sing. Some can paint well and others can do other things."

"Bobby can run very fast!" David stated.

"Yes, Bobby is a very fast runner. Perhaps when he gets bigger he will play football or baseball. Each one of us can do something well. We must remember that we are different from one another but that each of us is good for something."

Note: The teacher may choose to follow the story with a discussion on the things that make each one a special person.

SUPPLEMENTARY IDEAS

Have each child draw a self portrait at the beginning and end of the year. Keep to examine later. The pictures reveal growth and maturation of the child. This exercise also helps the child become aware of all his body parts.

Listening exercise: Have the children close their eyes. Tell the class to listen to the number of times you make a certain sound. (clap hands, tap pencil on table, snap fingers, etc.) This is good to help the child to develop concentration.

Fun activity: Let the children clean table tops with scented shaving cream. This is great for the sense of touch and smell. Give each child a small amount of shaving cream and let him spread it on the table. They may draw with fingers if they choose. This activity should be used on formica top tables or desks.

Discussion: Discuss the importance of certain animals. (Example: bees pollinate flowers; frogs eat insects in gardens, etc.) Then discuss what each child in the room can do that is important and/or special.

Each child may relate to the teacher a story about himself. (What he likes to do; what he does when he goes home; what he did on a trip, etc.) The teacher writes his story out and later prints or types it on paper. The child may want to draw a picture to go with his story. The teacher could attach a school picture to the story and this could be a Mother's Day gift. The teacher may want to read the story to the class. This is good in the early part of the year as get-acquainted material.

ADDITIONAL IDEAS
(for teacher use)

COMMUNITY HELPERS
(Grocer)

The Grocer

POEM From him we buy all that we eat.
Our bread, our vegetables and meat.
He helps us any way he can.
Our grocer is a helpful man.

ARTS AND CRAFTS

Collage: make a collage from grocery labels.

Butcher apron: Use small white plastic garbage bag. Cut side seams. To form rectangle shape, cut 1"-2" strips from top to center (use the side strips for tie). Cut ½" strips about halfway down for neck ties. Cut across to form bib. These aprons can be used as paint aprons after grocer unit.

Paper grocery store: Fold the ends of a large sheet of newsprint to the center (this will be the doors of the store).

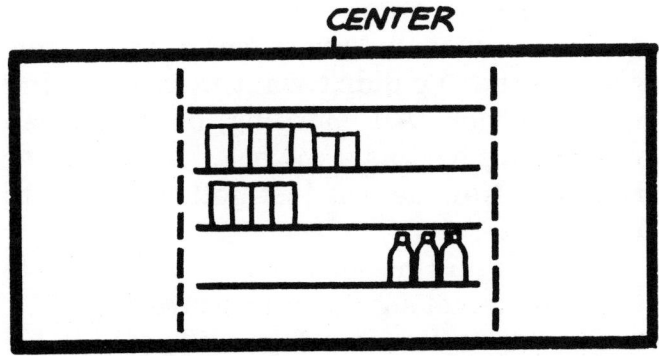

Grocery cart: Cut cart and wheels from construction paper. Attach wheels with brads. Pipe cleaner stapled on the corner is the handle.

Draw lines across center section for the shelves. When folded, cut corners diagonally for the roof effect.

13

On front of folded paper each child will print his name above the words GROCERY STORE. Children can cut pictures of food products from magazines and paste on the shelves. They may also draw, color, cut and paste their own food products.

Four Little Butchers

FINGER PLAY

Four little butchers cutting up meat
(chopping motion)
The first butcher said "Meat is good to eat."
The second butcher said "This will be a treat."
The third butcher said "Wrap it up neat."
The fourth butcher said "Our meat can't be beat."

STORY

The Treasure Hunt

"Donnie," called Mother, "it's time to go to the grocery store."

Donnie was having such a good time playing that he didn't want to go shopping with Mother. All morning he had been pretending he was a cowboy, astronaut, or fireman. Now he was just getting ready to be a pirate.

"Well," said his mother, "if you want to be a pirate, let's go on a treasure hunt."

That sounded exciting. "What will we hunt for? Where can we look? How will I find it?" Donnie had so many questions that Mother couldn't answer quickly enough.

"We'll look for things to pack in a picnic lunch. When we get to the grocery store, I'll give you hints of what the treasures are. You will really have to think hard and open your eyes to see what you can find."

All the way to the grocery store Donnie was so excited. What fun shopping was going to be today!

"Now remember," his mother said, "if you want to find your treasures, you'll have to walk slowly along with me and put your things in the cart."

"Okay," said Donnie. He was ready to start.

"We'll start with an easy one," said his mother. "Look for something that starts out as a plant in the farmer's field. After it is harvested it is made into something we like for our sandwiches."

Donnie knew Mother was talking about bread. As he walked along with his mother he kept his eyes open and watched for the bread. When they came to it, Donnie picked out a loaf of bread carefully and put it in the cart.

"Good," said his mother. "Now see if you can think of something that is round, red and crunchy."

The first thing Donnie thought of was a ball but that couldn't be right. Who would want to eat a ball? Soon he noticed they were in the produce department. This is where all the fresh fruits and vegetables are kept. Donnie looked and looked before he saw the tomatoes. They were red, but not crunchy so he kept looking. Right down the counter, there was the biggest pile of shiny red apples that you have ever seen. Donnie knew now what his mother was thinking of. He helped her select some nice apples before going on to the next hint.

"You will have to find two things now," said his mother. "I need two things that we get from cows. Donnie knew right away that one thing he liked came from cows and that was milk. The other was a little harder and Mother had to give him another clue.

"We like to cook this when we go on a picnic."

What could Mother be thinking of? As they passed the canned fruit he knew that it wasn't there. Down the cereal row. No, you cook oatmeal but not on a picnic! Around the corner and back up the row with coffee and tea. No, that was for mothers and daddies. How about noodles?

"No," said his mother, "noodles are made from flour and eggs."

"I like peanut butter," said Donnie. "Is that it?"

"No, peanut butter is made from peanuts," said his mother.

Donnie thought hard. Suddenly he remembered. "Meat," he said.

"Yes," said his mother, "that's it. Let's go pick out some meat and then it will be time to go."

When they got home they put away the groceries.

"We will pack our picnic lunch now," said his mother. "We will use some of the food this little pirate helped me find. Maybe at the bottom of the treasure chest we will find some animal cookies for dessert."

Sure enough on the bottom of the treasure chest was the cookie box.

MUSIC

What Do I See in the Store?

(tune — "Here We Go 'Round the Mulberry Bush)

What do I see in the store, see in the store,
See in the store? What do I see in the store,
When I go each week?

I see fruits and vegetables in the store,
In the store, in the store. I see fruits and vegetables in the store when I go each week.

(repeat the first verse)

I see bread and butter . . .

(repeat the first verse)

I see milk and eggs . . .

(repeat the first verse)

I see meats and treats) . . .

SUPPLEMENTARY IDEAS

Visit a grocery store. It is fun to give each child a particular item to look for as they tour the store.

Make a grocery store in the classroom, using empty containers. Let the children role play (1) a shopper, (2) cashier, (3) a sacker, (4) a butcher. Children can make paper money to use in play.

ADDITIONAL IDEAS

(for teacher use)

COMMUNITY HELPERS
(Postman)

The Mailman

POEM The mailman is a most funny chap.
He dresses in blue and wears a cap.

He smiles a lot and seems quite happy.
In fact he reminds me of Grandpappy.

He carries a bag slung over his shoulder.
When he sees my dog he's suddenly bolder.

He carries more letters than you can imagine.
The ones that he gives me I have to examine.

I wonder where he gets all of that mail.
And if I ask, do you think he will tell?

The Postman

I see him coming down the street.
He's dressed in blue and looks quite neat.

He wears a cap and carries mail.
To homes through rain, sleet, snow or hail.

ARTS AND CRAFTS

Mail box: Use a piece of blue construction paper approximately 9" by 6". Fold each 6" end ½" and press down. To form front edge of box, fold these ends toward center until they meet and press (when opened you will have three sections). To make legs of box (optional) cut up ½" on the center folds and ½" up on the folds at end. Fold the parts inside and staple together. For the opening in the box, cut a 2" horizontal slit about ½" from the top. Cut down on each end ½" and fold outward. Put glue on the ½" folds on ends and attach to another piece of paper.

For top of the mailbox, fold red construction paper into 4½" x 6" size. Glue the back 4½" side to mounting paper where blue bottom is glued. Bend red paper into arch and glue front edge to the front of the box. It will be necessary to hold this a few minutes until it dries. (you may want to staple instead of glue) Print U.S. MAIL across the box.

Note to teachers: This is not as complicated as it sounds. Five-year-olds can do quite well with step-by-step procedure. For the younger child make a flat blue rectangle and paste to the paper. Add a red semi-circle at the top.

ACTION POEM

(three children are required for action)

Postman

Drop your letter in the slot.
Where does it go?

Postman looks at the address.
I'll bet he'll know.

He sends it on to Grandma.
Happy she'll be.

To get a special letter.
That day from me!

STORY

Randy Visits The Post Office

Randy was watching his mother wrap a package that she would send to his grandmother.

"Mother, how will grandmother get her package?" asked Randy.

"We'll take it to the post office tomorrow and they will take it to her," said his mother.

"But how?" asked Randy.

"The best way to understand how it's done is to ask the postman to show you tomorrow," said his mother.

Randy was eager to go to the post office the next morning. He had been there often but this time would be special.

"Mr. Garcia," Randy's mother said to the post office superintendent, "can you show Randy how this package will get to his grandmother?"

"I'll be glad to," said Mr. Garcia. "Come with me, Randy."

Randy followed Mr. Garcia to the back where the mail was sorted and sent to other parts of the United States. There were big baskets everywhere. Randy saw the carriers sorting mail into slots in a shelf-like structure.

"See these large baskets?" Mr. Garcia asked as he pointed to the large baskets set on rollers.

"Yes, sir," answered Randy.

The numbers above the basket are zip code numbers. After we put stamps on your package, we'll check the zip code to see where the package will go."

"My package will go in this one," said Randy. He pointed to the middle basket.

"That's right," said Mr. Garcia. "This basket has the same zip code as your package."

"What happens next?" asked Randy.

"Each day a big truck stops by this post office and collects the letters and packages. The truck delivers the mail to other cities," said Mr. Garcia.

Randy followed Mr. Garcia out a double door that led to a ramp. Men were loading mail bags onto a truck.

"This truck is getting ready to leave now," said Mr. Garcia. "It will take mail to cities and towns North of here. The truck which will take your package will be here later today."

"Does the truck go to my grandmother's house?" asked Randy.

"No, it will go to the post office in Central City. The postman at the post office there will sort the mail for delivery in that city. There will be a carrier who will deliver the package to your grandmother."

"Gee, there are lots of people who help get the package to my grandmother," said Randy.

"Yes, Randy," said Mr. Garcia. "there are many people who work to deliver your mail."

"Thank you, Mr. Garcia, for showing me how the mail is delivered. I think I will be a postman when I grow up. Delivering mail is an important job."

SUPPLEMENTARY IDEAS

Visit a post office. Children enjoy mailing a letter to a parent or friend.

Let children pantomine postman delivering mail to homes, sorting mail at post office, selling stamps at the counter.

Discuss the pictures which appear on stamps.

ADDITIONAL IDEAS
(for teacher use)

COMMUNITY HELPERS
(Fireman)//
Our Friend, The Fireman

POEM He drives a big truck that is painted red.
If he hears the alarm he jumps out of bed.

He is very fast and he is so ready.
It's no wonder they call him
  "Ready Freddy!"

If ever there's a fire, I'll know who to call.
That "Ready Freddy", he's always
  "on the ball"!

ARTS AND CRAFTS

Fire truck: Cut the fire truck on the fold of red construction paper. Attach wheels with brads. The ladder can be made from spaghetti, straws or pipe cleaners. Fireman figures can be stapled onto truck.

Fireman booklet: Children will decide the appropriate color for the fireman objects. They can cut each square and staple into a booklet. (illustration on this page and next)

Fire hydrant: Paint empty thread spools with tempera.

Fireman

ACTION POEM

See all the firemen
Sliding down the pole.

When the firebell sounds,
Each fireman then bounds.

To the truck they run.
So fast it could stun.

Whee, whee, whee, whee, whee.
Now what do you see?

The firemen are here.
There's nothing to fear.

Water from their hose.
Makes sure the fire goes!

STORY

Tommy's New Bike

"Oh!" said Tommy when he saw his new bike. "It's so shiny."

Tommy's mother and dad were glad that he liked his birthday present. Tommy was six years old.

"Can I ride it now?" asked Tommy.

"First we need to get a license for it," said his dad. "We'll take the bike to the fire station. They will write down the serial number of your bike and issue you a license plate."

"Why do they take down the number?" asked Tommy.

"If your bike is stolen, the fireman can give the policeman the number of your bike so that he can help find it," said his dad.

"Gee, I didn't know firemen would do that for me," said Tommy.

"Yes," said his dad, "the fireman is an important helper and a very good friend."

SUPPLEMENTARY IDEAS

Take the children on a tour of a fire station.

After the visit to the fire station, children can pantomine what firemen do.

Discuss with the children what to do if:
(a) you see a fire down the street.
(b) you see another child playing with matches.
(c) you discover that your own house is on fire.
(d) you smell smoke in your house.

Discuss the usefulness of fire:
(a) to heat the home
(b) for cooking
(c) to get rid of waste
(d) in factories
(e) in industries
(f) in camping

ADDITIONAL IDEAS

(for teacher use)

COMMUNITY HELPERS
(Milkman)

The Milkman

POEM The milkman drives a great big truck
And brings us milk and butter.
He comes twice weekly to my home
Before going to another.

Milkman

Who's helping the milkman?
Now I'll give you a clue.
If it's not Mr. Jones
Then it is someone new.

He'll read the note Mom left.
That says, "Please-milk-one quart."
He puts it by our door.
He's such a helpful sort.

Have you guessed who it is?
The reason that I know.
That helpful girl is me.
The milkman told me so.

ARTS AND CRAFTS

Milk carrier: Attach a pipe cleaner onto a plastic strawberry basket to use as a carrier. Milk bottles can be made from tissue paper rolls and covered with white, brown, or orange construction paper. Pill bottles filled with colored water could also be used.

Ice cream cone: Use brown construction paper to make the cone. Stuff a ball of cotton on top for the vanilla ice cream.

Collage or mobile: To make children aware of dairy products, make a collage or mobile of dairy products (i.e. milk, cheese, ice cream, etc.)

STORY

The Mystery of the Missing Milk Bottle

Every other day the Powell family ordered three bottles of milk from the milkman. Before the family wakes up, the milkman arrives at their front door and puts three bottles of milk by the door.

At seven o'clock the mother comes to the front door, gets the milk and takes it to the kitchen. Each child gets a glass of milk for breakfast. There is Susie Powell, Tommie Powell, and baby Kellie.

One morning Mrs. Powell went to the front porch to get the three bottles of milk. But when she reached for the milk there were only two bottles. "Gee," said Mrs. Powell, "I just know I told the milkman to leave three bottles this morning."

Mrs. Powell forgot about the missing milk bottle until two days later when she went out to get the three bottles of milk. Just like the last time one bottle was missing. There were only two bottles!

"Someone must be taking a bottle of milk before I come out for it," Mrs. Powell thought. "Who can it be?"

When Mrs. Powell served breakfast that morning, she told the children about the missing milk bottles.

"I bet a green slimy monster took the milk," said Tommie.

"There are no slimy monsters in our neighborhood," said Mother.

"Maybe Tabby Cat knocked over the bottle and licked up the milk," said Susie.

"But, if Tabby Cat did that," said her mother, "the empty bottle would be there."

"This is really a mystery," said Mr. Powell.

All the children except Kellie (she could only coo and babble for she was a baby) tried to solve the mystery of the missing milk bottle.

The morning of the next milk delivery, the Powell family was on watch. There were four faces (baby Kellie was still in her crib) peering out the front window. At six o'clock, just like always, the milkman arrived. He put three bottles of milk on the front porch and left to deliver milk to the rest of the neighborhood.

The family waited to see what would happen. They waited and waited. It seemed as if nothing would happen when

... (the children must decide who was taking the milk. This is a good creative activity for the children.)

SUPPLEMENTARY IDEAS

Visit a dairy farm if possible.

Discuss the many products which are made from milk.

Mix ingredients together for homemade ice cream. Use an electric freezer to freeze ice cream. When ready serve a small dish to children.

Mix instant pudding and serve to children.

ADDITIONAL IDEAS

(for teacher use)

COMMUNITY HELPERS
(Policeman)

Guess Who?

POEM He stands at the corner and helps us
    cross the street.
He is dressed in blue and he's always
    very neat.

When I grow up I'd like to be just like
    this man.
I'll wear a uniform and help all that I can.

I'll help children cross the street
    and old people too.
And maybe someday I'll even get to
    help you!

Policeman

Who's your friend in the big blue car?
You see him most every day.
He will always try to help you.
If you ever lose your way.

He checks homes with a watchful eye.
He might help us cross the street.
We all may need him by and by.
In fact he's quite nice to greet!

    Who is he?

ARTS AND CRAFTS

Safety: Use scraps of plain-colored fabric and magic markers and dowels (cardboard cylinders from coat hangers make sturdy dowels) to make flags. Let children draw various traffic signs (i.e. stop, slow, etc.) on fabric. Staple to dowel. Use to reinforce safety rules, playing traffic policeman, going on a trip, etc.

Policeman's badge: Cut shape from cardboard. Cover with foil. Attach with pin or double face tape.

Game: Billy is lost. Help the policeman find Billy's home by tracing the route he must take.

SUPPLEMENTARY IDEAS

Invite a policeman to visit. Discuss how policemen are our friends. Dramatize policemen helping children cross the street (children take turns being policeman).

Play little lost boy or girl. Policeman asks child, who is crying, if he's lost. This encourages the child to know name, address and phone number because this will help policeman to find the lost child's home.

Form an avenue in the classroom. Let a child use a tiny whistle and help the children cross the street, using his hands in giving directions. Some children can be cars; other can be pedestrians.

Stress the importance of not getting into a car with a stranger or for taking candy or gum from strangers.

ADDITIONAL IDEAS

(for teacher use)

COMMUNITY HELPERS
(Baker)

The Baker

POEM Who bakes our bread and dresses in white?
The baker of course. He does it right!

He gets up early before sunrise.
To work the dough is an exercise.

He'll shape it into loaves, buns and rolls.
For doughnuts he'll have to leave
 some holes.

Then we get to go to buy his bread.
How lucky we are to be thus fed!

ARTS AND CRAFTS

Bread truck: From one slice of bread, cut off crust and curl two slices to make wheels. Cut a large rectangle for the body, and a cab is shaped from the remaining rectangle. Round one corner for the cab. Attach with toothpicks. Raisins may be placed on center of wheel for hub.

Construction paper baked goods: Cut circles in various sizes to represent cookies, pies and cakes. Let the children add other colors to make their baked goods (i.e. brown spots for raisins or chocolate cookies; red spots for cherries in pies, etc.) Decorate cakes for birthday parties. Squares and rectangles could be used for cakes and bread. Use "baked goods" in play store. This is a good time to introduce dozen, half dozen, etc.

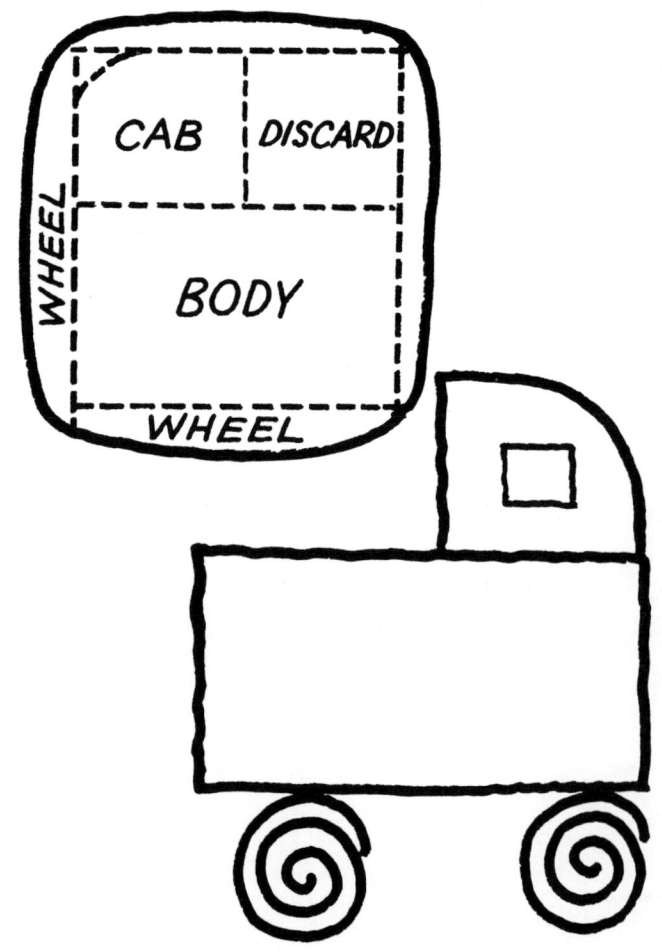

The Baker

ACTION POEM

The baker works the dough.
And then he lets it rise.
He beats it down just so.
It has to grow in size.

The baker rolls it out.
Using his rolling pin.
Shapes it without a shout.
And lets it rise again.

The baker lets it bake.
And waits a little while.
Not too long does it take.
It always makes him smile.

STORY

A Visit to the Bakery

Julie's mother and dad own a bake shop. Often she takes cookies to her classmates at school. One day her mother said, "Julie, next Wednesday is Valentine's day, would you like to invite your friends at school to come and visit the bakery?"

"Oh, yes, Mother, that would be fun," said Julie.

That day Julie told her teacher that her mother and dad would like to have the class come to the bakery and see how bread, cookies and cakes were made. The teacher made plans for the class to ride the bus across town to the bakery.

Everyone was so excited when Wednesday arrived. They boarded the bus and rode to the bakery.

"We're almost there," said Julie as she pointed to the small white building with a red-lettered sign which read "STEWART'S BAKERY".

"Welcome, children," said Julie's mother.

Mrs. Stewart led the children through the bakery showroom into the kitchen.

"Umm, something smells good," said one of the children.

"That's fresh bread just taken from the oven," said Mrs. Stewart. She pointed to six loaves of bread on a nearby table.

"They're not sliced!" said one of the boys surprised.

"The bread you buy in the grocery store is sliced by a machine," said Mrs. Stewart. "But the bread we bake here is sold unsliced. Some mothers like to slice their bread thick and some slice their bread thin."

The children's eyes grew big as they looked around the room. There were shelves with big bags of flour, sugar, baking powder, salt and flavoring. There were long tables where the baked cookies and cakes were iced. The children liked that table best!

"Today," Mrs. Stewart began, "I'm going to show you how to make cookies."

"Yippee," shouted the children.

Mrs. Stewart led the children to the long mixing table. They stood around the table and watched while Mrs. Stewart began putting dry ingredients into a large bowl. She put flour, salt and baking powder into the bowl and mixed it together, she rolled the dough out flat onto a cloth-covered board and cut it with a round cookie cutter. She placed the round pieces of dough onto a cookie sheet and put it into the oven to bake.

While the cookies were baking, Mrs. Stewart told the children how to make bread and cakes.

"The cookies are ready," said Mrs. Stewart. "Please find a place around the icing table and you can decorate your own cookie."

The children worked excitedly as they created an unusual design on their cookie.

"We'll take the cookies back to school and eat it during snack time," said their teacher.

As the children left the bakery, they said "Thank you, Mrs. Stewart, thank you."

What an exciting morning the children had at the bakery!

SUPPLEMENTARY IDEAS

Let children use playdough and form into baked goods; rolls, bread, doughnuts, etc. Have rolling pin and baking pans available.

Visit a bakery

Give the children a sugar cookie to decorate with ready-to-use icing.

Let the children taste flour, sugar, salt, vanilla and shortening. Illustrate how different these things taste when we mix them together. If possible, make cookies, bisquits or cupcakes. If no cooking facilities are available, the teacher should have prepared a finished product ahead of time so the children can sample it.

Response poem: Children can fill in the rhyming words.

See the baker rolling the dough!
What he is making, I don't know.

O, goodness! Now it starts to bake.
Do you think it could be a *cake?*

What smells so good? Oh, me! Oh, my!
Do you think maybe it's a *pie?*

It's almost done so now we'll see.
Cookies and bread for you and *me!*

ADDITIONAL IDEAS

(for teacher use)

THANKSGIVING UNIT

The Pilgrims

POEMS   The Pilgrims came to this great land.
They came to worship freely.
They came — these few under God's hand.
They came escaping tyranny.

I Wish

I wish I might have lived
A long, long time ago.
And been a young Indian
With the name of "Little Crow."
I might have gone a-hunting
With a strong, young Indian brave.
Gone off into the woods, the fields
Or perhaps even a cave.
I could have worn bright feathers
And used paint upon my nose.
I could have had beads round my neck
Moccasins round my toes!

The Past

Indians lived here in the past
On this very spot I'm told.
They saw the hills, the woods, the trees
And felt the wind, so cold.
I wonder if some Indian girl
Had any thoughts like mine.
And sat under this very tree
To while away the time.

ARTS AND CRAFTS

Make a turkey from construction paper. Children cut feathers and attach to large circle. Smaller circle makes head; triangle, the beak.

Popcorn turkey: Children follow teachers directions and illustration. (1) draw a circle (2) draw his head inside the circle (3) draw two small circles for his eyes (4) draw a triangle for his beak (5) draw three feathers on top of the circle (6) draw two legs and feet under circle (7) give each child a handful of colored popcorn. With white glue, let them glue the popcorn on the tail feathers. (Older children can save out 4 or 5 red kernels to glue on for wattle.)

Turkey planter: Color small styrofoam cup brown. Cut outline shape of turkey head (on fold).

Glue toothpick in between the heads. Fill cup with dirt and let children plant a cutting of a geranium. If it has nice leaves, these can serve as tail feathers. Otherwise, use colored toothpicks stuck in cup. Stick turkey's head in front of cup.

Indian pendant: Cut a cardboard circle (or any shape) to desired size. Glue assorted macaroni into design on cardboard. Spray gold. Punch hole in top and put yarn through for the chain.

Indian vest: Cut out side sections of large brown grocery sack. Make hole in bottom to fit over child's head. Cut 1"-3" fringe around the open end of the sack. Using side panel scraps, cut two 1½" wide strips to staple to front and back panels (under arm) to hold vest together.

Pilgrim man's hat: Cut an 11" diameter circle from black construction paper. In the center cut out a hole 5½"-6" to fit child's head. Cut a 6" wide strip of black construction paper approximately 24" long (may need to piece). Crease one of the long edges about 1". Staple at ends, then attach the creased end to the circle at hole. Add a buckle at front (3" square with center cut out) to front of hat.

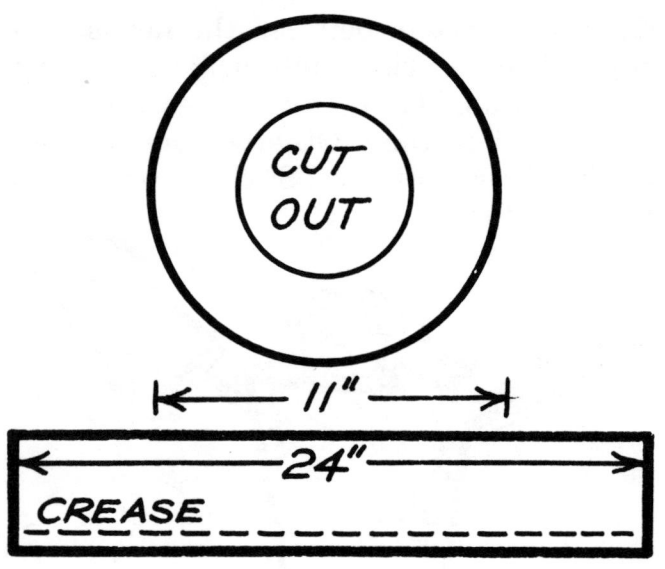

Pilgrim man's hat

FINGER PLAY

Here's an Indian

Here's an Indian with feathers a-bending

And here is his teepee on the ground

When the wind flies by,
His feathers fly high,

So he jumps in his teepee like a hound!

MUSIC Indians

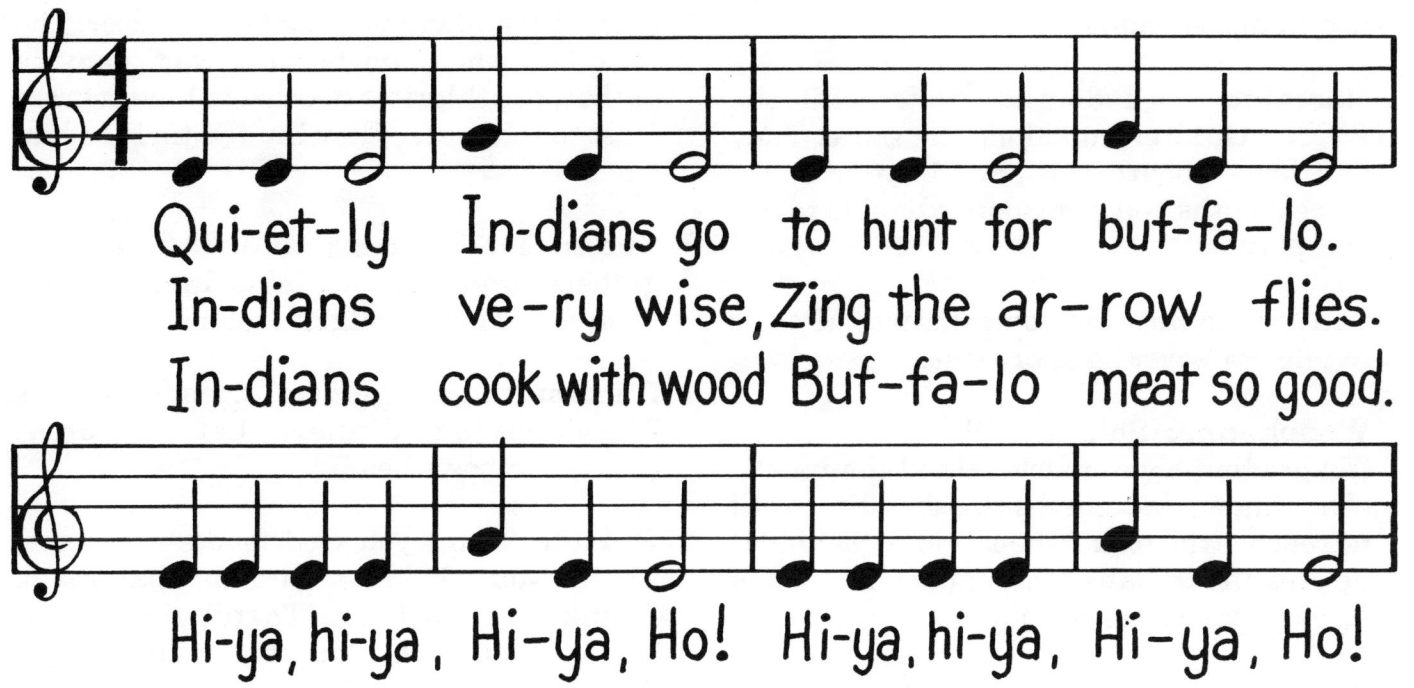

PLAY

A Thanksgiving Story

CHARACTERS: Wahpohanna (Indian boy)
Daniel (pilgrim boy)
4 pilgrim boys and girls
4 pilgrim men and women
3 Indians
Indian chief
(Note: number of non-speaking parts may vary according to need)

PROPS: (Optional) Box covered with brown paper for rock. Mural of ship on water for background. Indian dress for boys (headband, vest) Pilgrim hats for girls and boys (made from paper)

Narrator: Many years ago in early fall a ship called the *Mayflower* sailed from England in search of a new land to settle. They wanted to be able to worship as they pleased. The people on the ship were called Pilgrims. The ship reached the shoreline of what is now the Eastern part of the United States. When the ship dropped anchor, a group of Indian boys were watching with questioning eyes. They had never seen a ship like this. They continue to watch as the Pilgrims come ashore.

Scene I:

Behind a large rock, 4 Indian boys are watching the Pilgrims as they look around their new home. The Indian boys are dressed with headbands, vests made from brown paper bags and fringed around the bottom. Their faces may be painted.

Wapohanna: What strange people come from across water! (The other Indian boys nod in agreement.)

Narrator: The Indian boys watch while the Pilgrim children run along the shore. They had been aboard the ship *Mayflower* for three months and were glad to be able to run and play.

2nd Indian boy: Boy come this way. (Points to pilgrim boy who approaches.)

Wapohanna: Shh! Be still.
(The Indian boys crouch behind the rock.) (The Pilgrim boy climbs the shoreline until he reaches the rock. When he looks behind it he sees the Indians. The Indians kneel and stare at the white boy.)

Daniel: Hello ... I'm Daniel (points to himself)

Wapohanna: How! (raises hand). Me Wapohanna (point to himself.) You on board big boat. Where you come from?

Daniel: I have come from across the ocean, a place called England. Where you live?

Wapohanna: (Stretches hand out behind him). Forest.

Daniel: You and me be friends. (Motions to Indian, then himself.)

Wapohanna: (He nods) We be friends.

Daniel: I must return to the others. Come and visit me soon. (He moves away and waves goodbye).

Narrator: During the weeks that follow, the Pilgrims build log cabins and plant crops. Wapohanna and other members of the tribe become good friends with the Pilgrims and show them how to plant Indian corn and catch fish and kill wild turkey and deer. The next fall when the harvest was ready to gather, the Pilgrims decided to have a great feast to celebrate. They invited their Indian friends.

Scene II: Pilgrims and Indians are gathered around a long table. Plenty of food is on the table. A pilgrim man speaks.

Pilgrim man: Welcome friends to this Thanksgiving dinner. Let us pray. (Everyone bows head)

Unison: Thank you, God, for our new home. Thank you, God, for animals that roam. Thank you, God, for Thanksgiving day. Thank you, God, for the Indian ways. Amen.

Narrator: This was our first Thanksgiving. Each year since that time, America has set aside a day to be thankful to God for all our wonderful blessings.

Players may line in front of audience and take a bow.
The End

SUPPLEMENTARY IDEAS

Give each child an Indian name to use all week.

After discussing why Pilgrims were thankful, let each child tell something for which they are thankful.

Let each child make an "I am thankful" booklet.

ADDITIONAL IDEAS
(For teacher use)

A CHRISTMAS UNIT

Elves at the North Pole

POEM   Little hammers tap.
Little things they tag.
Elves are making toys.
To put in Santa's bag.

Up at the North Pole
While all of us sleep.
Small elves are working.
Not making a peep.

Dolls and teddy bears
Couldn't do without.
After Goodnight prayers.
That we'll dream about.

ARTS AND CRAFTS

My Special Friend

I have a special friend; he's as jolly as can be. You can guess who he is if you play this game with me. In the center of the paper draw a circle:
  Step 1.

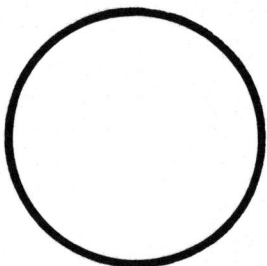

Draw a smaller circle for a mouth that says, "Ho, Ho!"
  Step. 2.

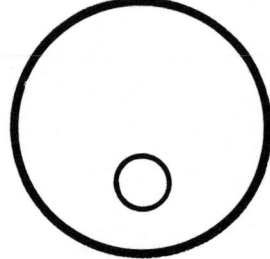

Above the mouth place a cute red nose and mustache white.
  Step 3.

To this face add the eyes that sparkle ever so bright.
  Step 4.

On top of his head draw a red hat with white trim.

Step 5.

Have you guessed that it's Santa? It really is him!

Draw a Santa holding a sack and put on the bulletin board. Let the children cut a toy from a catalog that he would like to receive. Paste onto a square of colored paper. Attach to Santa's sack.

Candle Holder . . . Invert a small aluminum pie plate. Glue thin red candle to bottom. Glue holly around base of candle.

Tree ornaments . . .
1. Make candy canes with white pipe cleaners and narrow strips of crepe paper or red garbage bag twisters.
2. Use plaster of paris in small mold. Before it is dry put a toothpick through top to make hole for hanging string. Children may paint ornament with thick tempera. When dry put a christmas seal on each side. Shellac or spray with clear lacquer or plastic. Use a gold cord or colored yarn and make loop to hang.

3. Picture rings . . . Cut two rings of construction paper. Place school picture on string and tape with clear tape on back. Put ends of string on one ring and paste the other ring on top of this. To cover tape on back, cover with Christmas seal. Teacher may write date in gold or red ink.

Card Holder . . . Make Santa in chimney from red construction paper.

I Can Be

FINGER PLAYS
ACTION POEMS

I Can be:
 As tall as a Christmas tree. (stretch tall)
 As round as Santa. (Circle arms in front)
 As tiny as an elf. (bend body to become smaller)

I Can:
 Bend like a candy cane. (bend head and neck)
 Look like a star. (stretch arms and legs in all dir.)
 Prance like a reindeer. (Prance around the room)

Five Little Elves

One, two, three, four, five little elves.
Putting toys on Santa Claus' shelves.
First little elf had something blue.
'Twas a small ballerina shoe.
The second elf had something red.
It was a little girl's doll bed.
Third little elf had something white.
It was a truck shiny and bright.
Fourth little elf had something brown.
It was a funny talking clown.
Fifth little elf had something black.
It was his very own knapsack.

Ten Little Reindeer

(Tune is One little, two little, three little Indians.)

MUSIC

One little, two little, three little reindeer.
Four little, five little, six little reindeer.
Seven little, eight little, nine little reindeer.
Ten little Christmas reindeer.

Christmas Choral Reading

CHORAL READING

Chorus: Christmas is a time of merriment.
All things start to look magnificent.

Small group: But what is Christmas all about?
What makes everyone sing and shout?

Chorus: Christmas is a time of great, great joy.
Gifts will arrive for each girl and boy.

Small group: Why are there gifts for us at all?
Why a Christmas tree in the hall?

Chorus: We are celebrating Jesus' birth.
He was God's son living on this earth.

All together: Let's celebrate Christmas with good cheer.
Love those at home and those that are here!

STORY

Christmas at Grandma's

Tim and Sue were so excited because they were getting ready to go to Grandma's for the Christmas holidays. It was always such fun to spend the holidays there.

"I hope they wait until we arrive to chop down the tree," said Tim.

"I want to find one that's as tall as the ceiling," said Sue.

Both children remembered last year at Grandma's. After breakfast on Christmas Eve morning, they went with Grandpa into the woods behind the farm and looked for a tree to chop down and to carry back to the farmhouse.

"Come on," shouted Mother. "We're ready to go to Grandma's."

The children were ever so excited during the drive. They laughed and sang to pass the time. Soon they neared the turn-off to the farm.

"We're almost there," said Tim excitedly.

It wasn't long before the car pulled up in front of the old farmhouse. Grandma and Grandpa were waiting for them on the front porch.

Tim and Sue hurried up the steps to the waiting arms of their grandparents. "Can we help find the tree?" the children yelled together.

Grandpa chuckled. "First thing in the morning we'll go out and find the loveliest tree you've ever seen," he said.

"Yippee," said Tim and Sue.

Bright and early the next morning Tim and Sue put on their heavy coats and their gloves. "Let's go," Sue said to Grandpa.

"Okay. Just let me get the axe," said Grandpa.

Off went the three into the woods behind the farmhouse. Tim and Sue looked at this tree and that tree hoping to find just the right one.

"How about this beauty?" asked Grandpa.

Tim and Sue tilted their heads back and gazed upward. "It's so big." said Sue.

"It's the biggest tree I've ever seen," said Tim.

"We'll take this one then," said Grandpa.

"It'll touch the ceiling for sure," said Sue.

After Grandpa chopped down the tree, Tim and Sue helped him drag it back to the house. "Gracious me!" said Grandma. "Will that fit through the door?"

"Isn't it beautiful?" said Sue jumping up and down.

"Just lovely," said her grandmother.

It was a tight squeeze but they finally got the tree through the front door and stood it up in the corner of the living room.

When it was up, Grandma brought a box and set it down on the floor. "We'll start making our decorations," she said. "There is felt, foil, glitter, string, paper and glue in the box. Your mother is popping corn now for us to string. We have a big tree to trim this year."

The children worked and worked. They made round balls with green and red glitter, silver bells, paper loops and many ornaments to hang on the tree. Last of all they strung the popcorn and placed it on the tree.

"Oh, how beautiful!" said Sue.

"It's such fun to trim a tree," said Tim.

"You did a good job!" said Grandma. "It's the loveliest tree I've ever seen."

SUGGESTIONS FOR USE: It would be appropriate to read the story before the children decorate the class Christmas tree. After the story have a box of paper, felt, string, foil, popcorn, etc., for them to make decorations. Also, story could be dramatized.

SUPPLEMENTARY IDEAS

1. Supply a box of scraps. Let children create a tree ornament for the class tree or for the family tree.
2. Make a collage Christmas tree out of various materials (examples; fabric, beans, corn, toothpicks, etc.)
3. Read the Christmas story out of the Bible. Refer to Luke 2:1-19. Allow children to dramatize.
4. Use groups of children to make the following shapes: (sitting on the floor would allow the onlookers to see and follow the outline better)
    a. a Christmas wreath
    b. a Christmas tree
    c. a Christmas tree ornament (hook and all)
    d. a star
    e. a longchain (they can interlock arms)

ADDITIONAL IDEAS
(for teacher's use)

HEALTH

Hygiene

POEM I like to brush my teeth
Each morning and each night.
For this will make them healthier
And keep them sparkling white.

I like to wash my face and hands,
And keep my hair well combed.
I like to practice cleanliness,
At school and at home.

ART AND CRAFT

Stick puppets: Make stick puppets of various objects in health unit study (foods, soap, toothpaste and brush, sunshine, etc.). Give one to each child. Go around the circle and let each child tell how he helps give us good health.

Toothbrush: A coffee stirrer colored or painted makes toothbrush when pipe cleaners are glued on. Cut pipe cleaners in thirds.

Doctor Kit: Paint a box black to resemble a doctor's bag. Print R.X. on the front. Inside include the following items: band aid (brown paper), square of gauze, stethoscope (made

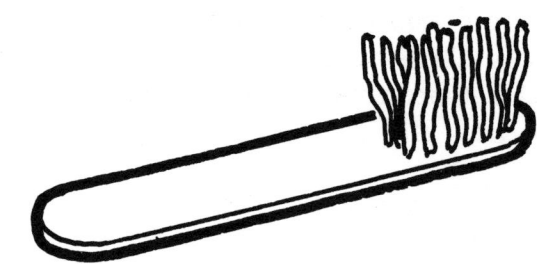

with 3 pipe cleaners and a spool), tongue depressor (popsicle stick), thermometer (clear straw and red pipe cleaner), ball of cotton, doctor headband with light (strip of construction paper and foil), nurse cap (white construction paper with red symbol).

Health

ACTION POEM Let's pretend that we are sleeping
Getting lots and lots of rest.
For good sleep helps all the children
Helps us act our very best.

When we rise let's eat a breakfast
That will help us feel just right.
Let's drink our milk and eat our food
And not leave a single bite.

Jumping rope and throwing soft balls
Is a way to have great fun.
Playing, "Let's follow the leader,"
Makes us skip and jump and run.

Stay Healthy
(Sing to "Row Row Row Your Boat")

MUSIC
Brush, brush, brush your teeth
Brush them every night.
Brush, brush, brush your teeth
Keep them shiny white.

Brush, brush, brush your hair
One hundred strokes at night.
Brush, brush, brush your hair
You'll keep it clean and bright.

Wash, wash, wash your face
Before you come to school.
Wash, wash, wash your face
That's our good health rule.

Sleep, sleep, sleep each night
You need to get your rest.
Sleep, sleep, sleep each night
You'll look and feel your best.

Play, play, play each day
Outdoors in the sun.
Play, play, play each day
Healthy children having fun.

STORY
Visit to Good Food Town

Billy was in bed. He had eaten too many sweets and had a tummy ache.

"Billy," his mother had said, "you must learn to eat foods which are good for you. I'll give you something to settle your tummy and then you can lie there and rest."

So here Billy was, lying in bed and wishing he had not eaten so much candy. When he went to sleep he dreamed he was in Good Food Town. At the entrance to the town was a sign which read:

"Welcome to Good Food Town;
The Home of Healthy boys and girls."

Billy entered Good Food Town and started down vegetable Lane. The first house he came to belonged to the carrot family.

"Hello," said Billy. "I know you. You're Mrs. Carrot. You are a vegetable that's good for my eyes."

"You're so right, Billy," said Mrs. Carrot. "You need yellow vegetables like me every day. I give you vitamin A and C."

Billy waved goodbye to Mrs. Carrot and contined on his way. He soon came to a group of lettuces playing ball.

"Hi," said Billy. "May I play too?"

"Sure," said the lettuce children. "We play ball here everyday. Along with good foods, exercise helps to keep our bodies healthy."

When Billy began to tire of the game, he said goodbye to his new friends and went down Dairy Street in search of something to drink. He was very thirsty after playing so hard. Soon he came upon a refreshment stand.

"May I serve you something cool to drink?" said the Orange who was behind the counter.

"What do you have?" asked Billy.

"We have delicious cold milk, orange juice, grape juice, pineapple juice and the specialty today is cranberry juice," said the Orange.

"No Cokes!" said Billy

"We serve only those drinks which are good for the body and keep us healthy," said the Orange. "Our drinks give you calcium and vitamins."

"I'll try the cranberry juice," said Billy. Billy took a couple of sips. "My, this is tasty. It tastes good and is good for me too. That's great."

Billy was discovering a lot of interesting things during his visit to Good Food Town. When he finished his drink, he decided to walk down Meat Blvd. He said hello to Mr. Fish who was rocking on his front porch; he waved to Mrs. Chicken who was feeding her chicks; he nodded his head when he passed by the Hamburger family who were taking their afternoon stroll.

Billy knew about the value of meats. His mother had told him that meats help build strong muscles. Since Billy wanted to play ball in little league next summer, he always ate his meat at dinner.

Before leaving Good Food Town, Billy took a stroll down Bread Alley. At the first house he heard laughter and talk so he peered through the window. It looked like a family reunion. He saw all the bread family: White Bread, Rye Bread, Wholewheat Bread and Raisin Bread. There were also cousins to the bread there too. The cereals, rice, macaroni and grits were all there having a good time.

"Please join us," called Mrs. White Bread.

"Thank you," said Billy. "I'm on my way home, I've learned a lot about good foods since I've been in your town. I've learned that I should eat vegetables for vitamins and minerals; dairy foods for calcium and vitamins and meats for protein."

"What about the bread family? Don't forget about us," said Mrs. Macaroni. "We supply carbohydrates to keep you from getting tired as well as iron and vitamin B. You should eat us everyday too."

"I'll remember that," said Billy . "I must go now."

Billy waved goodbye to his friends. Suddenly he felt someone shaking him. When he opened his eyes, he saw his mother.

"How do you feel, son?" she asked.

"Much better," said Billy.

"Do you feel like eating dinner?" his mother asked.

"Oh yes," said Billy. "I want to eat all the good foods that you have fixed for me. I know that I must eat these good foods to build a strong and healthy body. I'm not going to eat any more sweets. Oh, maybe just a little now and then!"

SUPPLEMENTARY IDEAS

Have a doctor, nurse and dentist visit the class.

Good health chart: Let the children keep a daily record (for one week) of their health habits. Include washing face and hands, brushing hair, brushing teeth, eating a good breakfast.

**ADDITIONAL
IDEAS**
(for teacher use)

HOLIDAY UNIT
HALLOWEEN

Halloween

POEM

At this time of the year we'll see scary things:
Ghosts, goblins, and witches and scary beings.

It's a fun time for all to scare each other.
Let's put on some masks and go scare my brother.

You be a white ghost and I'll be a black witch.
You wait by the fence while I hide in the ditch.

My gracious, he's coming. You see what I see?
I think he's that big cat that's headed toward me!

ART

WITCH: Cut a 2" diameter circle for face. Draw features on face. Paste a piece of yarn at top of the circle and a triangle hat on top of the yarn. Add a doubled piece of black construction paper cut for 3-dimensional nose. Paste head on popsicle stick to use as puppet.

PICTURE: Let children draw a picture of Wanda the Witch. (See story, Wanda the Witch)

FINGER PLAY

Five Black Cats

Five black cats are sitting on a gate.
The first one said, "The witch is so late."
The second one said, "It's dark tonight."
The third one said, "We will cause such fright."
The fourth one said, "Halloween is fun."
The fifth one said, "Get ready to run."
Five black cats are sitting on a gate.
One, two, three, four, five cats just can't wait.

Wanda The Witch
(tune — This Old Man)

MUSIC   Wanda the witch has eyes of green
The wart on her nose makes her look so mean.
She doesn't need a broom to fly through the air

Her flying machine takes her everywhere.

She flies high and she flies low
She flies wherever she wants to go:

She flies east and she flies west
She hardly ever stops to rest.

She is ugly, grouchy and fat
A black cat clings to her tall, tall hat.

Wanda the witch is a sight to see
She makes Halloween a treat for you and me.

STORY

Wanda The Witch

In the deep dark forest near the town of Timbergrove lives a fat old witch named Wanda. Now Wanda is no ordinary witch. For you see, instead of riding a broomstick, Wanda rides a flying machine.

Every Halloween night, or so folks say, Wanda the Witch emerges from the deep dark forest. She flies over the countryside in her most unusual flying machine.

Legend has it that Wanda the Witch did not always have this flying machine. Many Halloween nights ago all the young witches of the deep dark forest outside Timbergrove decided to play a trick on Wanda the Witch.

The young witches did not like Wanda because she was fat, ugly, and grouchy. Besides that, she had a big wart on the tip of her nose which made her look very mean. When the young witches teased her about her ugly nose, she would shoo them away with her broomstrick.

On one particular Halloween night the young witches played a trick on old witch Wanda. While she was preparing for her nightly cruise that Halloween, they stole her faithful broomstick and hid it where she would never find it.

"My broom! Where's my broom?" Wanda the Witch screamed when she discovered her faithful companion was not in its usual place.

Wanda the Witch was furious. If she couldn't find her broomstick, she wouldn't be able to fly around the neighborhood and scare the children of Timbergrove.

When the other witches flew out of the deep dark forest that night, Wanda the Witch was still looking for her broomstick.

"Drats!" said Wanda the Witch and stomped her foot. "I'll not be left behind."

Quickly she began to assemble odds and ends into a huge pile. In a flash she constructed the most unusual machine anyone has ever seen. When it was finished, she leaned back on her heels, twitched her nose, waved her hand and presto the machine began to make a roaring sound. Wanda the Witch put on her big pointed hat, grabbed her black cat under her arm and jumped onto the seat of that most unusual flying machine and away she flew.

Needless to say Wanda the Witch was the talk of the town of Timbergrove. She made quite a sight as she flew over the treetops that Halloween night.

Every Halloween night since, the children of Timbergrove meet in the town square as soon as it is dark and wait for Wanda the Witch to fly over in her most unusual flying machine.

SUPPLEMENTARY IDEAS

Give the children pre-cut triangles, circles, squares, and rectangles. Let them paste on a sheet of white paper and complete a Halloween scene with crayon. (Example: A cat may be made with a rectangle body and a triangle head. Add legs, ears, whiskers with a crayon.

What sounds do these make:
   (a) witch
   (b) ghost
   (c) cat
   (d) squeaky door
   (e) bat

Make Halloween characters using balloons, felt pens and pieces of construction paper. Blow balloons (black for witch, orange for Jack-o-lantern, etc.) and draw the faces with felt pens.

HOLIDAY UNIT
ABRAHAM LINCOLN

Abraham Lincoln

POEM Abraham Lincoln was honest and strong.
He served his country well and so long.

He could split many logs so all were told.
In body and mind Abe Lincoln was bold.

ART

BRACELET: Ask children to bring 3-6 pennies. Let them shine them with copper cleaner. (Vinegar and salt or an eraser will also clean pennies.) Cut a piece of clear Contact and press. Adjust bracelet to slip on child's wrist.

SUPPLEMENTARY IDEAS

Pantomime scenes from Lincoln's life such as cutting logs, reading by candlelight, etc.

Make a beard from black construction paper. Attach to face with tape or string.

After reading a story about Abraham Lincoln (particularly his life in a log cabin) ask the children what things they might have missed if they, too, had lived back in the time of Abe Lincoln.

VALENTINE

A Valentine

POEMS Take lots of lace and a red heart,
And put it all together.
And write on it, "Here is my heart!"
And I'll love you forever!

Valentine's Day

Valentine's Day is the nicest day of all!
It comes in the winter which comes after fall.

It's that time of year when we send out some notes.
We send out our Valentines in envelopes.

All our friends want to know if we still love them.
Is our love so true or is it just a whim?

So let's send each other this message so true . . .
To all of our friends we'll say, "I do love you!"

ARTS AND CRAFTS

VALENTINE HOLDER: Cut two 8" paper plates into heart shape. Staple plates together, leaving top open. Decorate. Attach string for hanging. Print child's name on front and hang.

VALENTINE CARD: Fold red construction paper. Cut out a white heart (or use white doily) and paste on front. Print verse:

Someone loves you
Do you know who?

Take a look inside and see
The one who loves you is me.

Inside paste a picture of child. (Use school picture or Poloroid picture.)

VALENTINE WATCH: Make a watch from construction paper. Glue (or staple) strip to fit over wrist. Cut out valentine shape to glue to strip with numbers written on it. Attach two construction paper hands with brads.

BRACELET: Make the same way as watch, but without numbers. More hearts may be added to bracelet. "I love you" may be written on center of heart.

FINGER PLAY

Five Little Valentines

Five little valentines just for you
The first one says, "My love is so true."
The second one says, "You have my heart."
The third one says, "Let us never part."
The fourth one says, "Won't you please be mine?"
The fifth one says, "'Til the end of time."

MUSIC

A Valentine
(tune — Skip to My Lou)

I have a valentine just for you
I wrote on the card, "I love you true."
I wrapped it and mailed it yesterday.
Close to your heart I hope it will stay.

STORY

Antonio's Surprise

Antonio was very unhappy. Today was the day his class was to have its valentine party. Antonio was sick and had to stay home.

"We'll have a party here," said his mother cheerfully.

"It just won't be the same," said Antonio sadly.

That day when the children met in their classroom, they were very excited. Only one girl noticed that Antonio was missing. Everyone liked Antonio and was sorry he could not be at the party.

"What can we do to share our good time with him?" one of the boys asked.

"Let's save some of our valentine cookies for him," suggested one friend.

"I know another thing we can do," said Sondra. "We can make a giant card for him and all sign it."

"Yes, let's do that," said the children.

They began to make the card. It was so big they had to make an envelope to put it in. Everyone had such fun.

"Antonio will like that," said their teacher. "I'll take the card, his valentine box and his cookies to him this afternoon. It was sweet of you all to think of Antonio. That is really a gift of love."

SUPPLEMENTARY IDEAS

Explain to children how to cut a heart. Fold the paper and cut out a shape resembling an ice cream cone. Give each child a piece of paper and allow him to create his own valentine.

Cut heart shape pieces of bread and decorate with icing.

GEORGE WASHINGTON

POEM

George Washington

George Washington was our first President
Honest and strong and a very nice gent.

We'll always remember George Washington
Who fought many battles until he won.

ART

CHERRY TREE: Give each child an outline of a tree. Let children cut cherries from red construction paper. Paste to tree.

SUPPLEMENTARY IDEA

Look for coins or bills with a picture of George Washington.

Read a brief story about George Washington and ask the children which personal characteristics they noticed in the story (i.e. What did you like best about George Washington?)

GROUND HOG DAY

POEM

Ground Hog Day

This furry friend might come out once a year
To see his shadow if the day is clear.

And on this very special Ground Hog Day
If his shadow is seen, winter will stay.

For six more long weeks we'll have to keep warm.
We'll thank the Ground Hog for his quiet alarm.

ART

GROUND HOG PICTURE: Ground hog is mounted on popsicle stick. Cut slit in ground so you can push animal in and out of hole.

SUPPLEMENTARY IDEAS

Be sure to explain what happens if Ground Hog sees his shadow.

Let the children go outdoors and see their shadow.

Make shadow pictures with hands using a projector light.

Use the projector light to illustrate idea of ground hog seeing his shadow.

ST. PATRICK'S DAY
The Tiny Leprechaun

STORY

In Ireland, so folks say, there lives a tiny Leprechaun. No one has seen him but they know he's there because of the mischievous things he does. Legend tells us that anyone who can catch him gets his pot of gold.

Every night the mischievous two-foot tall man plays a joke on the townspeople.

One time he stuffed cotton into everyone's shoes. When they got up the next morning, they couldn't put their feet into their shoes.

The tiny Leprechaun was forever playing a trick on the townspeople.

"This trickery must end," declared the mayor one day.

He passed a decree that all the families of the town must make a special effort to catch the Leprechaun.

This was not easy because the Leprechaun never appeared until everyone was fast asleep.

The members of the families would take turns sitting in the living room at night to wait for the Leprechaun to appear. Every night the Leprechaun waited until the person on watch was asleep before he would come inside.

Each morning when the families awoke, they would know that the Leprechaun had been there for something mischievous had been done.

The Leprechaun's favorite trick was to put salt in the sugar bowl.

"Oh, how terrible my cereal tastes," the children would yell when they took a mouthful of salty flakes.

There was no doubt that the Leprechaun had been busy again.

One night, Shawn, the smallest member of the Irish town, decided to take his turn on watch.

"I'll keep my eyes open and catch the Leprechaun," he promised.

"You're too little to sit up and wait for the Leprechaun," said his mother. "Besides, you will surely fall asleep as soon as it is dark."

Shawn would not give in. That night he waited and watched but the Leprechaun didn't appear. Shawn decided to pretend to be asleep and trick the Leprechaun into coming inside.

He leaned back in the big arm chair and closed his eyes. Sure enough the Leprechaun came out from his hiding place and started his mischief making.

"I've caught you," said Shawn sitting up in his chair.

"Oh, no!" said the Leprechaun. "You have spoiled my fun and now you will have my pot of gold."

After that night, the Leprechaun was never seen again. Shawn was a hero of the town and shared his treasure with the other boys and girls.

ART

HATS: Make hats with large sheets of newsprint and decorate with shamrock.

LEPRECHAUN EARS: Make pointed ears from green construction paper for children to wear. Staple two pieces together around outer edge.

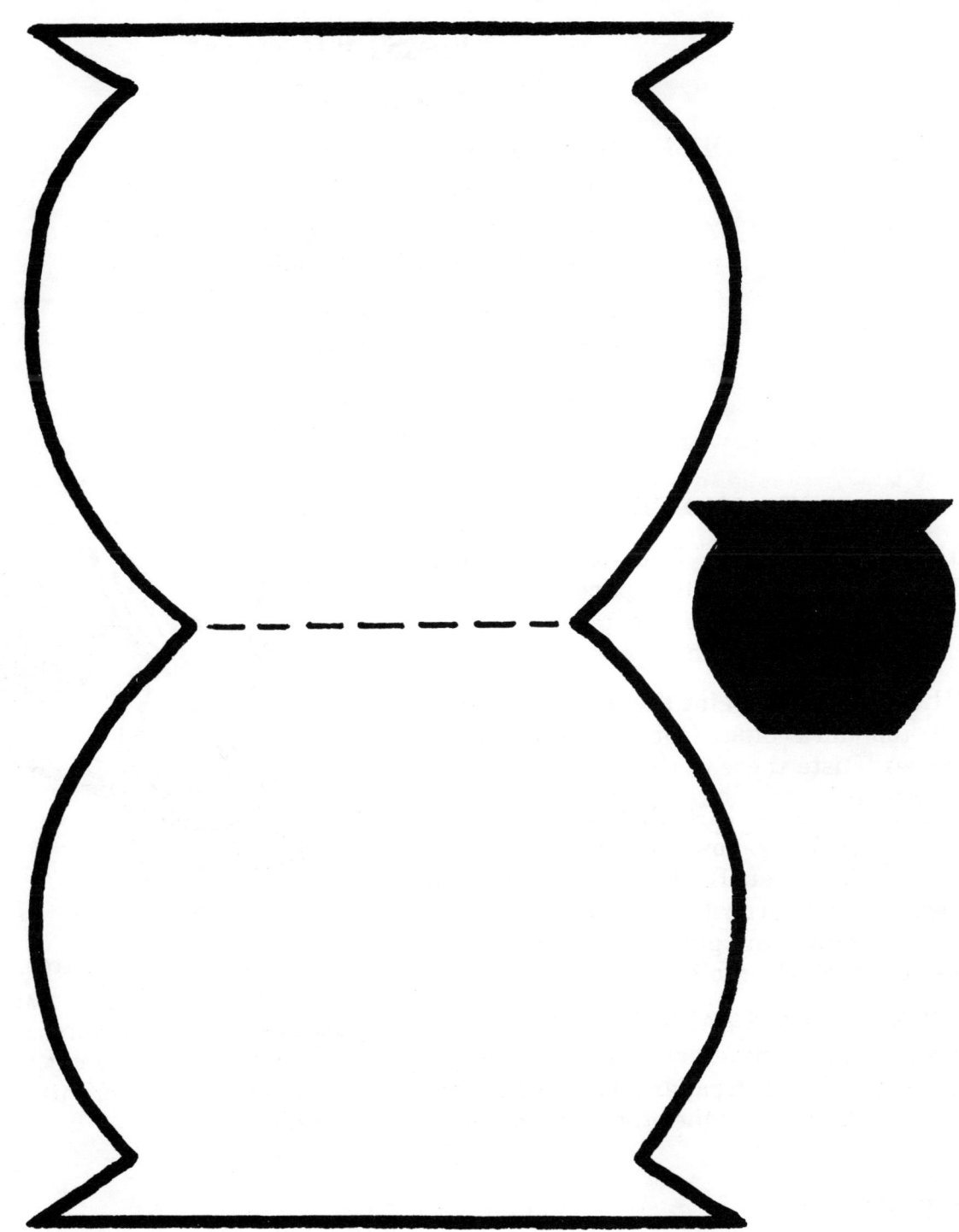

POT OF GOLD: Make a black pot from construction paper. Let children cut coins from yellow construction paper.

SUPPLEMENTARY IDEAS

Serve green punch.

Look for four-leaf clovers in the grass.

EASTER

Eastertime

POEM	Now Eastertime is almost here.
Who'll bring the eggs is not quite clear.

They say that eggs come from a hen.
Well, where has Mr. Rabbit been?

To find our eggs he's been somewhere.
Perhaps his secret he will share.

Well, anyway we'll have great fun,
While Mr. Rabbit's on the run.

ARTS AND CRAFTS

DECORATE EGG: Decorate a L'eggs Hosiery egg with contact paper, felt pens, etc. Teacher may wish to put a surprise inside and tape together.

SHADOW BOX: Paint the inside of a shoe box top dark blue. Cut out three white crosses. Paste these to the lid.

BABY CHICK IN EGG SHELL: Dip ball of cotton into dry yellow tempera. Make eyes with black felt pen. Beak can be made from a piece of black construction paper cut in triangle shape and glued onto cotton. Glue the cotton chick into half an egg shell.

BUNNY EASTER BASKET: Cut a hole in a large cylinder container (as an oatmeal box). Tape top lid. Attach paper rabbit ears on one lid and paper feet on the other. Cut Kleenex tissue into 1½"-2" squares. Pinch together; paste onto container. Paste construction paper eyes and whiskers in place. Two 2½"-3" finger slits can be cut in back, about 1" apart to provide grip. Put artificial grass in container.

ACTION POEM

Five Little Easter Bunnies

Five little bunnies hopping all around
The first bunny said, "I'm going to town."
The second bunny said, "I'll hide the eggs."
The third bunny said, "I will stretch
   my legs."
The fourth bunny said, "I'll eat a carrot."
The fifth bunny said, "I'll scare a parrot."
Five little bunnies so soft and furry,
Ran around the yard in such a hurry.

MUSIC

The Easter Bunnies
(tune — Mary Had a Little Lamb)

The bunnies hop hop down the trail,
Down the trail, down the trail

The bunnies hop hop down the trail
Twitching their nose and wiggling their tail.

They carry baskets with many treats,
Many treats, many treats

They carry baskets with many treats
For every boy and girl they meet.

Bunny
(tune — Skip to My Lou)

Bunny, bunny, hop around
Here and there, over the ground.

Are you looking for a treat?
Juicy carrots you can eat.

Bunny, bunny, how you hop!
Fast and slow and then you stop.

Fur so soft and ears so tall
You're the finest pet of all.

STORY
Jack and Benny Bunny

Near Mr. Brown's farm lived twin bunnies named Jack and Benny. They were identical, both having soft, white furry bodies with a black spot on their left ear. The bunnies usually played together, but always made sure they didn't go in Mr. Brown's fields. Mr. Brown didn't like to see bunnies hopping on his vegetables and taking nibbles. Mother Bunny told her boys not to snack between meals, especially at the vegetable garden. But one day Jack was extra hungry since he had skipped breakfast, so he squeezed through Mr. Brown's fence and started munching on some cool, fresh vegetables. Benny followed after him to stop him, but Jack was already eating huge mouthfuls. Soon the farmer saw the two in the garden and came running after them. Benny and Jack raced to the fence. Benny squeezed through, but Jack got stuck halfway through the fence because he had eaten too much. Mr. Brown came up right behind the frightened rabbit and pushed him through with his large, *hard* boot. "Stay out of my garden!" he yelled. Jack's bottom was sore the next day, but he had learned his lesson.

SUPPLEMENTARY IDEA

COLLAGE: Make a collage from crushed egg shells. The egg shells may be colored or white. Children may make an original design or you may suggest that they make a bunny, chick, or cross.

SEASONS

Sleepy Animals

POEMS

All Winter do some animals sleep.
No clocks or appointments do they keep.

Some people call it "to hibernate."
I think that they just get up too late.

By the time they get up it'll be Spring.
And they'll want to eat up everything.

I wonder what Mom and Dad would say,
If I tried to eat and sleep this way?

Snow

Snowflakes falling gently to the ground.
Some are swaying; Some are going 'round.

They are twirling, tumbling backwards, too.
Just as if someone had said, "Shoo! Shoo!"

Soon all will be covered with the snow.
White up above and white below!

Signs of Spring

I think that Spring is everywhere.
Just try to smell it in the air.

All the flowers are now in bloom.
Their brightness scares away the gloom.

I see a bird building a nest.
Do you suppose he'll take a rest?

The trees are now starting to bud.
Soon all the limbs the leaves will flood.

Before too long we'll have showers.
It'll help your plants and it'll help ours.

I am happy that it is Spring!
Look, beauty is in everything!

ART AND CRAFTS

Fall leaves: Cut 1½" squares from a variegated tissue paper (fall colors). Wrap the paper around the end of a pencil, dip in glue and attach to picture of a tree. This gives a 3-D effect.

Fall pictures: Let the children paint leaves with orange, brown, yellow paints.

Line of snowmen: Fold newsprint lengthwise. Cut on fold to have two pieces. Fold the piece end to end, holding fold toward you. Fold twice more. The teacher may draw on the folded part a "surprise snowman". The child will cut along the lines, being careful not to cut hands. Unfold to find four snowmen holding hands.

Icicles: On the top of a dark piece of paper paint a line of white tempera. Let the children blow gently with a straw so the paint will run. The results looks like icicles.

Trace John as he goes down the hill on his sled. (see the attached sheet)

Basket of Spring flowers: Let the children cut out a flower basket (mimeographed). Give the children several pieces of pastel construction paper and let them draw and cut out some flowers. Staple, paste or tape the basket onto another piece of paper, allowing for a 3-D effect. The children can glue the flowers behind the basket.

Vinyl flowers and basket: Let the children cut flowers and baskets from vinyl wallpaper. (sample wallpaper books can be obtained from decorator shops) The children will enjoy arranging the flowers on the baskets.

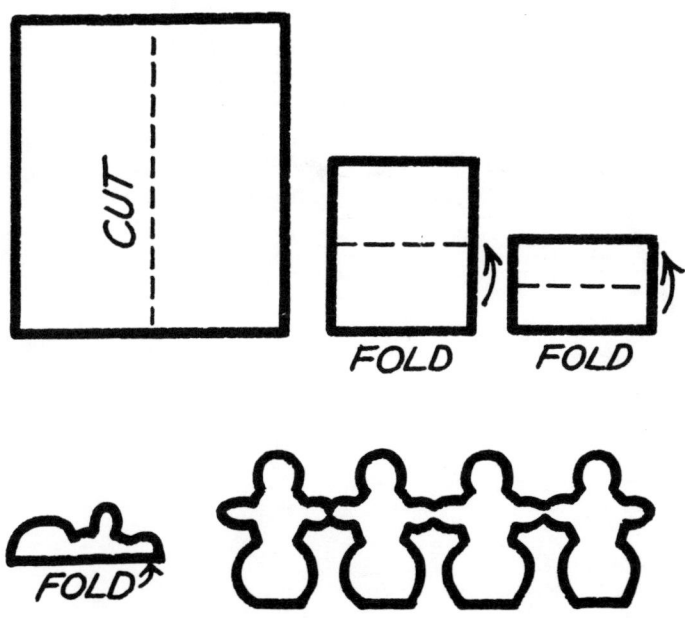

Winter booklet: During your unit on Winter let the children draw pictures illustrating Wintertime. You may include: 1) trees without leaves; 2) snow scene on black paper. Use white chalk; 3) snowflakes. Use white chalk on light blue paper; 4) children building a snowman; 5) skiing.

Caterpillars: The curved pieces of packing foam make ideal caterpillars. Colored pins with round heads can be used for the eyes and antenna. Lay the caterpillar on a leaf where holes have been punched.

Cocoon: Cover a peanut with yarn for a cocoon. Attach to a twig.

John is sledding down a hill. See if you can help him stay in the path. Watch out for the snowman and the pine tree!

Butterflies: Use a pipe cleaner for the body and variegated tissue paper for the wings. Sheer fabric, dipped in liquid starch and dried can also be used for the wings. The starch will give the wings body.

ACTION POEMS

Seasons

Flowers bloom; birds like to sing.
This always happens in Spring.

Then its Summertime once more.
We sift the sand on the shore.

In the Fall to school we're bound.
As the leaves fall to the ground.

Mr. Cold Wind starts to blow.
For its Wintertime you know!

Five Snowmen

Five happy snowmen standing in a row.
The sun melted one, so very slow.
Four happy snowmen having lots of fun.
One ran indoors to hide from the sun.
Three happy snowmen jumping up
   and down.
One ran away without ere a sound.
Two happy snowmen sliding down a hill.
Both fell over and lay very still.

STORY

Footprints in the Snow
(a flannel board story)

Little Brave and his father Crooked Arrow were going hunting for deer. Snow covered the ground so Little Brave and his father had to find the deer in a particular way. Do you know how? That's right, they looked for footprints in the snow.

Now Little Brave and Crooked Arrow saw several types of footprints. You can help them find the footprints for deer.

The first prints they saw looked like this (put rabbit print on flannel board). Do you know what animal made these prints? The animal is small and lives underground. Some can hop great distances. Yes, these are the footprints of the rabbit. (Place a picture of a rabbit beside the prints).

Little Brave saw these prints next. (put the squirrels prints on the flannel board). Can you help Little Brave decide who made these prints? This animal is small, lives in a tree and stores nuts for the Winter. Who can tell me the animal that made these prints? Correct — these are footprints for a squirrel. (Put picture of a squirrel next to prints.)

Next Crooked Arrow found another set of footprints (put prints of a fox on the flannel board). The animal that made these prints has a long bushy tail, is a swift runner and is very sly. Do you know the name of this animal? It is a fox. (put the picture of a fox next to the prints).

Finally, Little Brave and his father saw these prints (put the deer prints on the flannel board). Crooked Arrow was happy. Do you know why? Yes, these are the prints of the deer. (Put a picture of a deer on the flannel board beside the prints).

The prints and outline shapes of the animals are included on this page and the following one.

STORY

Exploring Spring

"Wake up, wake up!" said Mother Bear to her cubs Stinky and Winky. "Spring has arrived."

The two fuzzy black cubs stretched their legs and rubbed their eyes. They had been asleep all Winter. When they were wide awake, they followed Mother Bear outside into the warm sunshine.

Mother Bear was glad to be able to stretch her legs. She sniffed the sweet smells of Spring.

"Spring is my favorite time of year," she said to her twin cubs.

The cubs were scampering about in the warm sunshine. Mother Bear could tell they were enjoying Spring also.

"Stay close beside me," Mother Bear instructed her cubs. "We'll walk through the woods and enjoy Springtime."

Mother Bear took Stinky and Winky down to the stream.

"Watch how I catch a fish," their mother said.

Mother Bear scoopped her paw into the cool stream. When she brought her paw out of the water she held a fish.

"That looks easy!" said Stinky.

The two cubs walked into the water and leaned over to look for a fish. Suddenly Stinky splashed Winky with water and the battle began. Mother Bear watched her cubs playfully splash one another. Pretty soon the cubs grew tired of their play and wanted something to eat. They tried over and over again to catch a fish but found it to be more difficult than it looked when their mother had done it.

"Come," said Mother Bear. "I'll show you something else good to eat."

Stinky and Winky followed their mother to a green bush covered with red berries.

"Each Spring this bush is covered with delicious berries," said their mother.

The cubs nibbled on the berries until their tummies were full. They were sleepy so they curled up on a soft patch of clover and went to sleep.

Stinky and Winky awakened refreshed and eager to continue their examination of Spring. Mother Bear showed them beautiful pink and yellow flowers and colorful butterflies.

"I like Springtime," said Winky.

"Springtime is a beautiful season," said Mother Bear.

All too soon the sun began to hide its face. Mother Bear led her cubs back to their den.

"Do we have to go in?" asked Stinky.

"Yes," said Mother Bear, "we'll enjoy Spring again tomorrow."

The Midnight Intruder

Summer had finally arrived. The Cannon brothers were going on a camping vacation in the Rocky Mountains. When Wayne, Jim and Tom and their dad arrived at the campsite, they set up their tent and arranged their cooking and fishing gear outside. That night three tired boys collasped in their sleeping bags.

"Who made this mess?" Bruce Cannon asked his sons when they awoke the next morning and came out of the tent.

The three boys stared in disbelief at their camp gear scattered everywhere.

"I don't know how it happened," said Wayne.

"Don't look at me," said Jim. "I didn't do it."

"That leaves you," said Mr. Cannon looking at his youngest son Tom.

"Gee, Dad, I didn't do it."

"Let's all pitch in and get this camp cleaned up. We can't leave it in this mess while we're out fishing."

Once their camp was in order, Mr. Cannon and his sons ate a hearty breakfast and set out for a day's fishing on the upper Rio Grande River.

That night after a profitable day of fishing the foursome hit the sack early and didn't stir from their tent until daybreak.

"Boys!" Mr. Cannon yelled.

Each boy emerged from the tent still sleepy-eyed to find the camp in shambles again.

"Oh no, not again!" the boys said in unison.

"Someone must be coming into camp while we're asleep," said Mr. Cannon.

"But who could it be?" asked Tom. "We're so far away from civilization there's not another camp within miles of us."

"We'll rig a surprise for our nighttime prowler tonight," said Mr. Cannon.

Each boy offered his suggestion as to who the intruder could be. As they set the camp back to order once more, they made plans to surprise their mystery guest. That night after supper, the boys helped Mr. Cannon string a fishing line between two trees at the entrance of the camp. In another area, they stationed cans which they had filled with rocks. If the intruder entered the camp that night, he would make such a racket that the camp would be awakened. When preparations were completed, the foursome climbed into their sleeping bags to wait.

Eight o'clock; nine o'clock; ten o'clock; not a sign of their mystery intruder. By eleven o'clock everyone was fast asleep. Perhaps no one would come tonight.

About midnight the boys sat up with a start. Clang! Bang! The intruder had stumbled into the traps set for him. Mr. Cannon jumped up and went cautiously to the tent door. When he rolled back the flap and peered outside, he chuckled. The boys tumbled out of their bags and joined their father at the tent door.

"So that's our mystery friend," said Jim.

The large brown bear, not disturbed the least by the noise, finished brousing through the camp. Finding no food, he strutted out of camp, leaving it again in shambles.

The Seasons
(sing to tune — "Little Brown Jug" or "Humpty Dumpty")

MUSIC Tell me what you like to do
There's a season just for you.
Do you like to slide or skate?
Winter time is really great!
Baseball games; kites in the air.
Signs of Spring are everywhere.

Trips to the beach are so much fun.
In the bright warm summer sun.
Last of all remember fall.
Back to school for one and all.

SUPPLEMENTARY IDEAS

Discuss signs of Fall: Include dried colored leaves, bare trees, cool breezes, pumpkins, Halloween, football games, birds flying South and haystacks. Where possible take the children on a walk. Point out the signs of Fall.

Pantomine: Squirrels gathering nuts for Winter, leaves floating to the ground, raking the fallen leaves and putting in basket, birds flying South.

Make snow ice cream: In climates where snow falls, gather fresh, clean snow and mix some ice cream for the class. Add milk, sugar and vanilla to the snow.

Icicle popcicles: Freeze plain water in long narrow popcicle molds. Let the children enjoy these at snack time.

Match pictures: Have pictures of the following and match with the appropriate season: Snowman, bare tree, shower, beach scene, rainbow, snowflake, leaves, sun.

ADDITIONAL IDEAS
(for teacher use)

CIRCUS AND ZOO UNIT

POEMS

At the Circus

The circus is a wonderful place
Where there are animals with much grace.

Dogs jump through hoops and do it
   with speed.
Oh, its a wonderful life they lead.

Elephants dance and skip to a song.
You can believe they don't do it wrong.

The lion tamer snaps his whip so loud.
While the lions stare back, their
   faces proud.

Clowns come along with funny faces.
And with each other they run races.

Look, a lady who walks a tight rope!
She's up so high! She won't fall, I hope.

Down to the left a man's eating fire.
If I did that I think I would tire.

In a circus there is much to see.
That's why I'm so glad that you brought me!

My Visit to the Zoo

I'm always glad to visit the zoo.
And what I've seen I'd like to tell you.

One great big animal liked to hop.
With his babe in his pouch he would
   flop. (kangaroo)

Another animal was all black.
A sign on his bars said, "This is Jack."
   (panther)

There was an animal with a hump.
A ride on him might make me go
   "bump". (camel)

At another place I saw an ape.
I surely hope he doesn't escape. (ape)

I saw two animals with long necks.
The spots on them couldn't be called
   specks. (giraffe)

There was an animal with a trunk.
He also had a great deal of spunk. (elephant)

Oh, let me tell you the zoo is neat!
To get to go is quite a nice treat!

ARTS AND CRAFTS

Complete the animal pictures. Provide pictures of zoo animals with a part of their body missing. Children complete the pictures and color. See the examples on the following pages.

Complete the animal pictures .. continued

Complete the animal pictures .. continued

Animal in a cage. Children may draw any zoo animal (or teacher can provide an outline of an animal) and color appropriate color. Paste the animal on to a styrofoam meat tray. Make the bars of the cage with pipe cleaners. (Shoe box can also be used as a cage.)

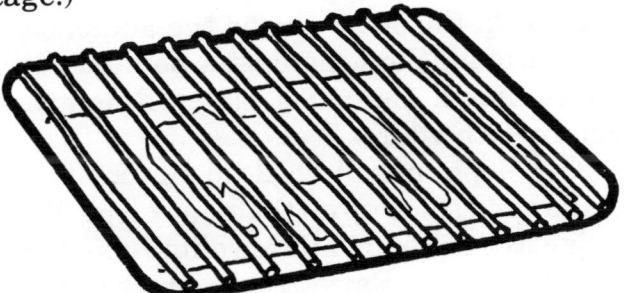

Handprint animals. Each child traces his handprint on to the paper. From the print he is to draw an animal that he might see in a zoo or at the circus.

ACTION POEMS
FINGER PLAYS

At the Zoo

One, two, three, What did I see at the zoo?
One, two, three, Guess when I give
   you a clue.

I saw an animal with a long neck. (giraffe)

I saw the king of beasts that gives a
   loud roar. (lion)

I saw a large animal with a long
   trunk. (elephant)

I saw a big cat with orange and
   black stripes. (tiger)

I saw a furry animal that hibernates in
   winter. (bear)

One, two, three, what do you see at the zoo?
One, two, three, give us a clue. We'll
   guess who.

(Give each child the opportunity to
   give a clue.)

The Funny Clowns

Guess who's coming to this town!
There'll be more than just one clown.

One and two. Oh, do you see?
That sad one makes number three.

Happy face is number four.
Oh, look now. Here come six more.

Number five's coat is all torn.
Next one likes to toot a horn.

Seven and eight are way in back.
They are pulling a big sack.

Here comes one with a small sign.
It says, "I am number nine!"

Last one coming throws a ball.
Waves and yells and says, "That's all!"

(This can be used as a fingerplay. See if the children can associate next, more, etc., with the actual number of clowns so far. Or, let the children dramatize it. Children may also draw the clowns described in Poem.)

Five Little Clowns

Five little clowns standing in a row.

The first clown said, "It is time to go."

The second clown started running 'round.

The third clown said, "I'm going to town."

The fourth clown did a fast somersault.

The fifth clown drank a chocolate malt.

Five little clowns did tricks so funny.

Laughed so hard it tickled my tummy!

MUSIC

The Clown
(tune is "Three Blind Mice")

Look at the clowns.
Look at the clowns.

See what they do.
See what they do.

They are so funny; they make me glad.
They do their tricks but some look sad.
When I see them I say, "Not bad!"

Look at the clowns.
Look at the clowns.

STORY

Under the Big Top
(DRAMATIZATION)

I went to the circus and under the big top I saw three rings where the animals and people performed. (have three rings drawn on the floor or make rings with tape.)

The ringmaster directed our attention to the first ring. (Have ringmaster point with his whip.) In it I saw four performing dogs. They jumped through a hoop and walked on their hind legs. (Have four children be the trained dogs and act out the narration. One child can be the dog trainer.)

The ringmaster pointed to the center ring where the tightrope walkers were performing. (Have two children be tightrope artists. They can walk on a rope which has been placed on the floor and carry a balance stick.)

The audience applauded. (Children who are not in the show can be the audience.)

Last of all the Ringmaster pointed to the elephants in the third ring. (Ringmaster points with whip.)

The elephants climbed up on top of their stands and stood up on their back legs. What a sight! (Have four children climb upon large coffee cans . . . Raise trunks in the air . . . Arms held together for trunk.)

The audience applauded again!

NOTE TO THE TEACHER: This is a sample of what can be done with role playing in the circus unit. You may choose to vary the above program to fit your needs, desires, etc. Other acts may include: 1. jugglers, 2. lion tamers, 3. Horses.

To enhance the excitement and to create realism, simple props may be used. Children may plan ahead what they would like to be and help with prop making. Children can also make tickets to sell at the ticket booth.

SUPPLEMENTARY IDEAS

1. Visit a zoo if there is one available.
2. Have a circus day on which the children can dress up as an animal or a performer.

ADDITIONAL IDEAS
(for teacher's use)

TRANSPORTATION

POEMS

The Airplane

The airplane flies so very high.
Starts on the ground. Soars to the sky.

Sometimes I wish that I could fly,
And often wonder why can't I?

Oh, to be able to spread my arms,
Fly over cities; fly over farms.

I know just what I'll do instead.
No need for arms. I'll use my head.

To go on trips, I'll take a plane,
Won't feel the cold wind or the rain.

Transportation

I saw the train coming down the track.
A trail of smoke coming out its stack.
"Toot, toot," it said as it passed me by.
It carried some goods to satisfy.

I saw a plane flying in the sky.
It zoomed on by while I blinked my eye.
Wonder where it was going so fast.
Wherever it goes it won't be last.

I saw a small tugboat in the bay.
It made at least three trips on that day.
It was pulling a very big load.
To do its job it follows a code.

I saw a bus going down the street.
To ride on it would be such a treat.
I know that it goes from place to place.
The driver must see many a face.

ART

SAIL A BOAT: Cut shape from top of an egg carton. Pipe cleaners may be used to hold paper towel sails.

SAILBOAT may also be made out of plastic margarine tub. Sail can be made with popsicle stick and vinyl paper. Children could play with this in bath tub.

ROCKET: Cut out the shapes on the attached sheet. These are pasted to toilet tissue roll.

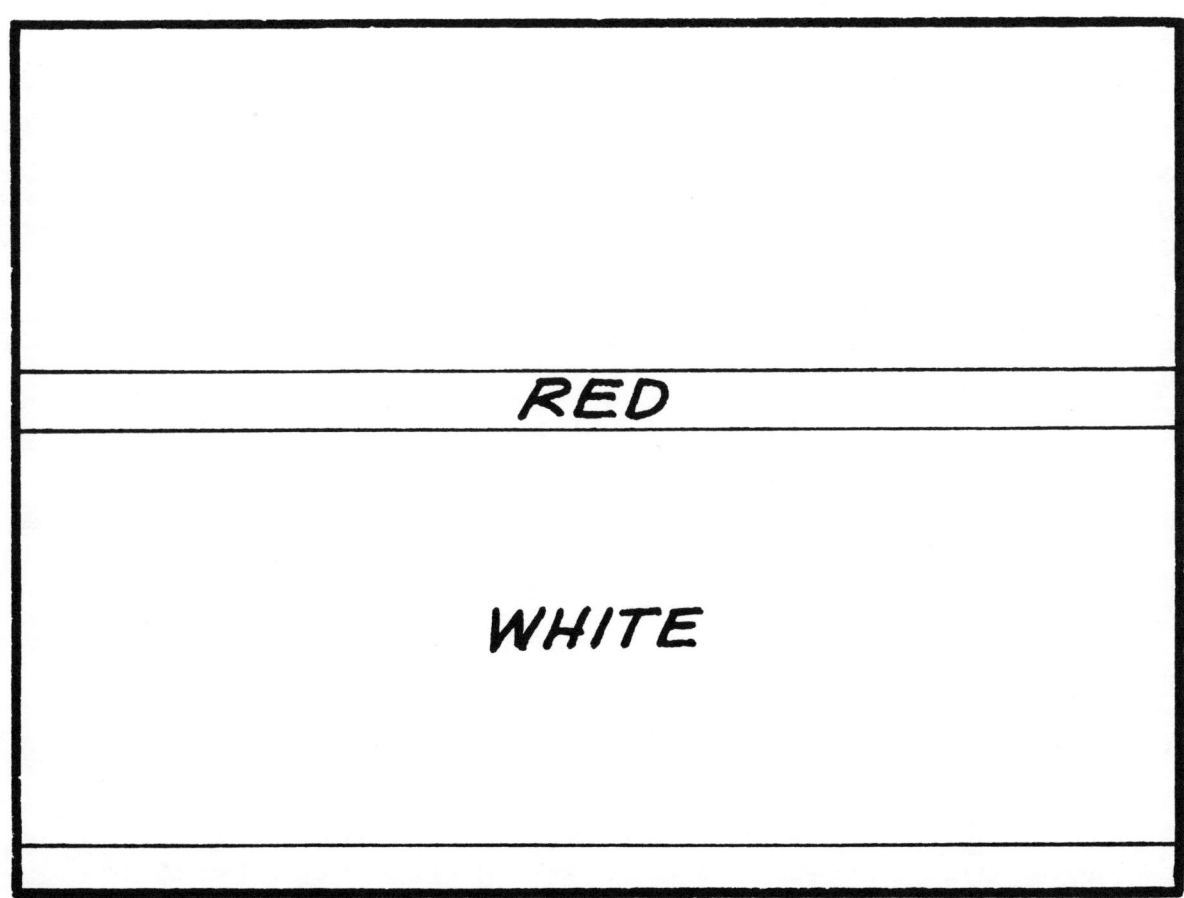

RED

WHITE

CUT AND GLUE TO TOILET TISSUE ROLL

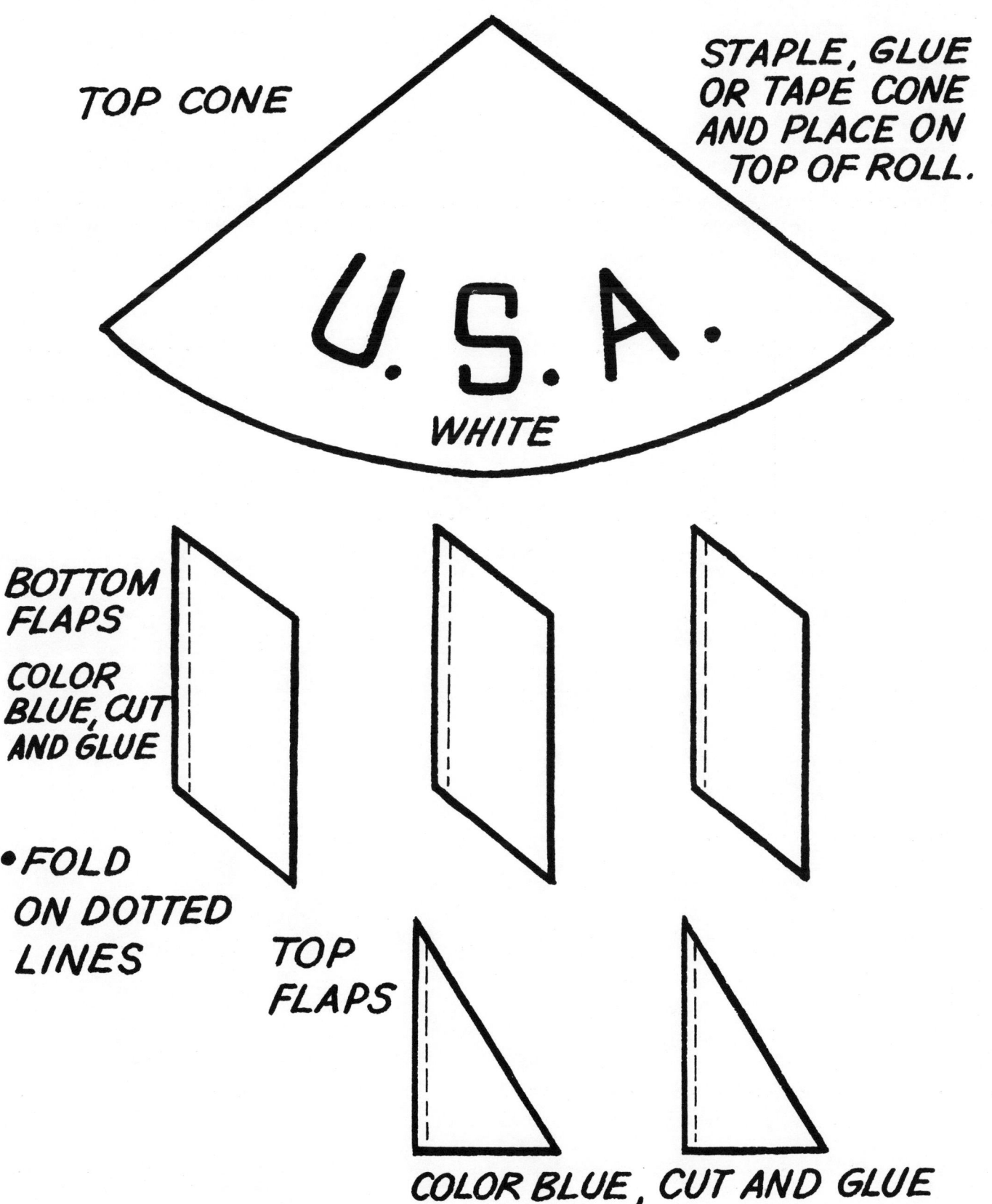

PAPER VEHICLES: Give each child two circles. Instruct the children to draw a vehicle that has wheels. This is a good exercise for drawing, cutting, and pasting.

PARACHUTE: Use scraps of thin fabric (square). (Handkerchief may be used.) Tie strings on each corner. Bring strings together and tie around a weight (rock, etc.).

ACTION POEM

Traveling

I walk on my legs. I ride my bicycle.
   (Fingers walk up arm; hands
     hold handlebars.)

I drive a small car. It's a fine vehicle.
   (Hands hold imaginary steering wheel.)

We go for a ride in a great big long bus.
   (Hands spread to indicate length.)

We wave at the people and they wave at us.
   (Wave)

I zoom in a plane at a very high speed.
   (Pass one hand fast, across front.)

My, but this is a ball. It is so, indeed!

Please watch as I paddle in my birch canoe.
   (Pretend to paddle.)

The water looks nice and the sky is
   pale blue.

These are just a few ways to get to a place.

Now let's try a train. We won't take up
   much space.

So, good-bye and so long to Mother and Dad.
   (Wave good-bye.)

We'll be back quite soon. There's no need
   to look sad!

MUSIC

The Train
(tune — "This Old Man")

The engine is coming down the track.
It is very shiny and black.

The coach is next and it is brown.
The people in it are sitting down.

The pullman is rolling in between.
It has many berths and this car is green.

The refrigerator car is cold and white.
Its food will be good to eat tonight.

The stock car's animals are for the zoo.
They are in cages. This car is blue.

The tank car is loaded (and it is yellow)
With gasoline for the service station fellow.

The mail car carries letters sad and gay.
It has packages and it is gray.

The caboose is always the last one, it is said.
We wave and wave. It is painted red.

STORY

Story of Transportation
(a flannel board story)

Hundreds of years ago man didn't have cars, jet planes, boats, or trains to travel by. Let your imagination go back to cave man times when man had only his feet to take him places. (Put picture of cave man on flannel board.) The cave man had to walk wherever he wanted to go. He probably didn't go very far. As he began to feel the need to visit his far-away neighbor, the cave man invented the wheel. It was a rough looking wheel, but it proved to be better than walking. (Put the wheel on flannel board.) As man became wiser, he made better wheels and used horses to pull them. (Put up picture of chariot.)

When the United States was settled, there were all kinds of vehicles with wheels pulled by horse or oxen. (Put samples of vehicles on flannel board — like covered wagon, stagecoach, buckboard.)

Pioneers traveled westward on the covered wagons. The farmers used the buckboard for carrying supplies to their farm from town. When people wanted to travel across country, they sometimes used the stagecoach.

After the United States began to grow and expand, the United States built a railroad across the country. The early trains were slow and had to have coal fed into furnaces to run. (Put picture of early train on board.)

In the 1890s people used bicycles as a means of transportation. Then in the late 1890s the first motor vehicle was built. (Show pictures of bike and Model T.)

Today we have many fast moving vehicles — cars, jet planes, speedboats, and rockets. (Display pictures of modern vehicles.) We have come a long way from the days when man walked wherever he wanted to go.

Discuss different means of travel by water, by air, on land.

By water	By air	On land
raft	balloon	car
canoe	blimp	truck
sailing ship	glider	train
steamship	airplane	motorcycle
barge	helicopter	bus
freighter	rocket	bicycle
speedboat		
tugboat		

SUPPLEMENTARY IDEAS

Display many kinds of toy vehicles. Discuss each, allowing children to contribute their thoughts. After discussion, let the children play with the toys.

Get several large boxes from the grocery store. Let children paint each box to represent the different cars of a train: black for engine, red for caboose, etc. Line these up in the room and let children take turns role playing the various train personalities.

Display pictures of the following means of transportation: truck, bus, car, train, plane, ship, rocket. Ask the following questions and let children decide which vehicle answers the question.
(1) Which one is used for going to the moon?
(2) Which one travels on tracks?
(3) Which one carries vegetables from farm to city?
(4) Which one goes through the air?
(5) Which one do we park in our garage?
(6) Which one stops in many cities and carries many people?
(7) Which one travels in the ocean?

CAVE MAN

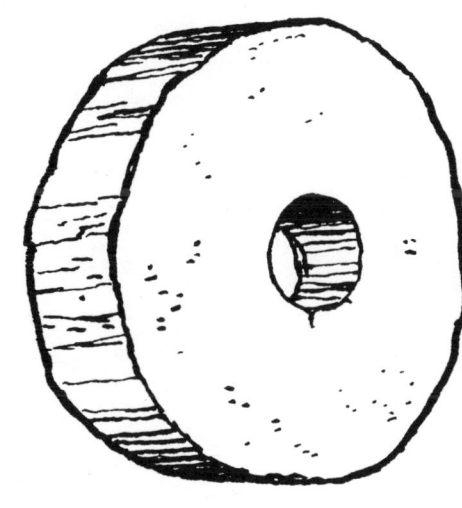
WHEEL

CHARIOT

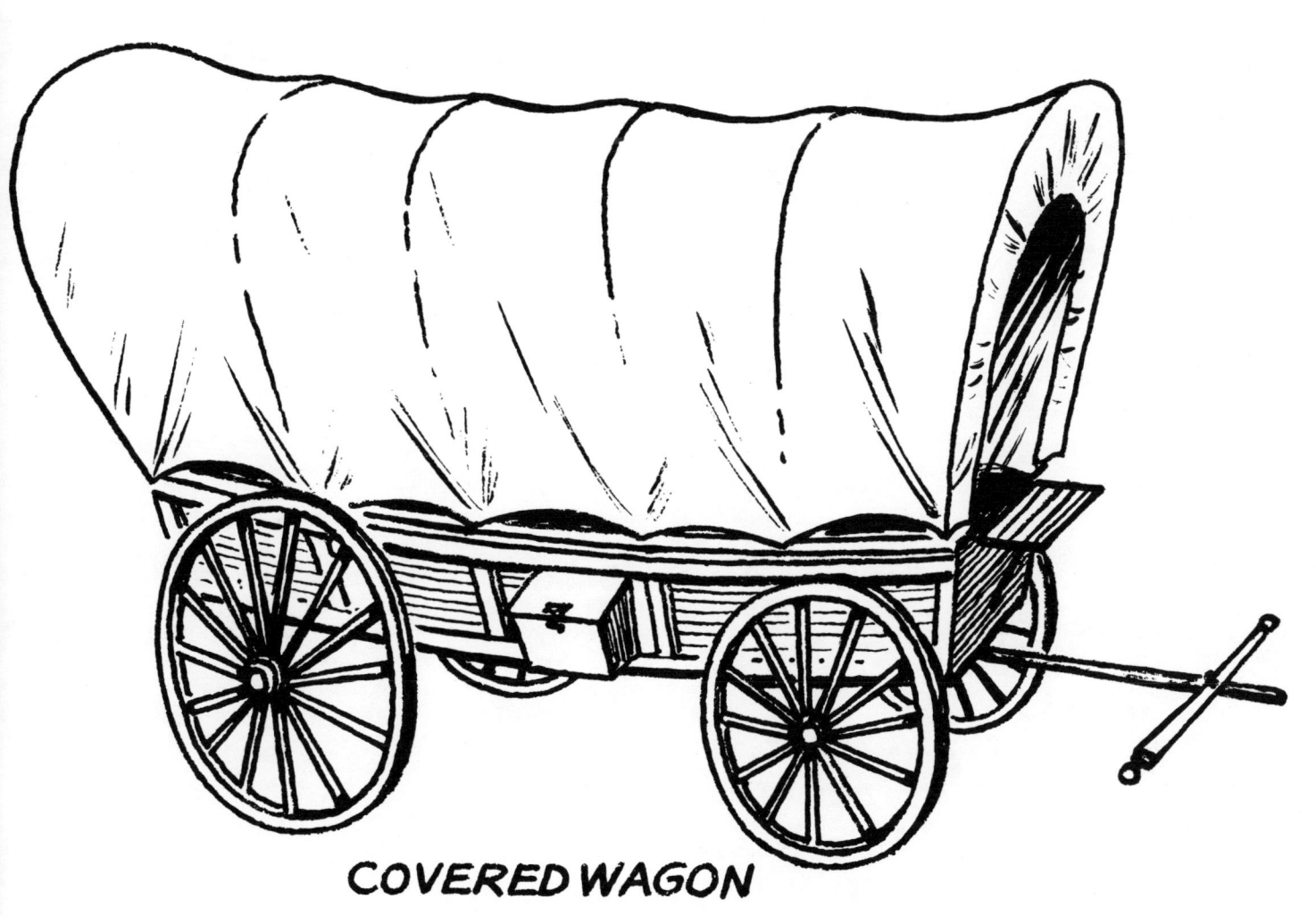

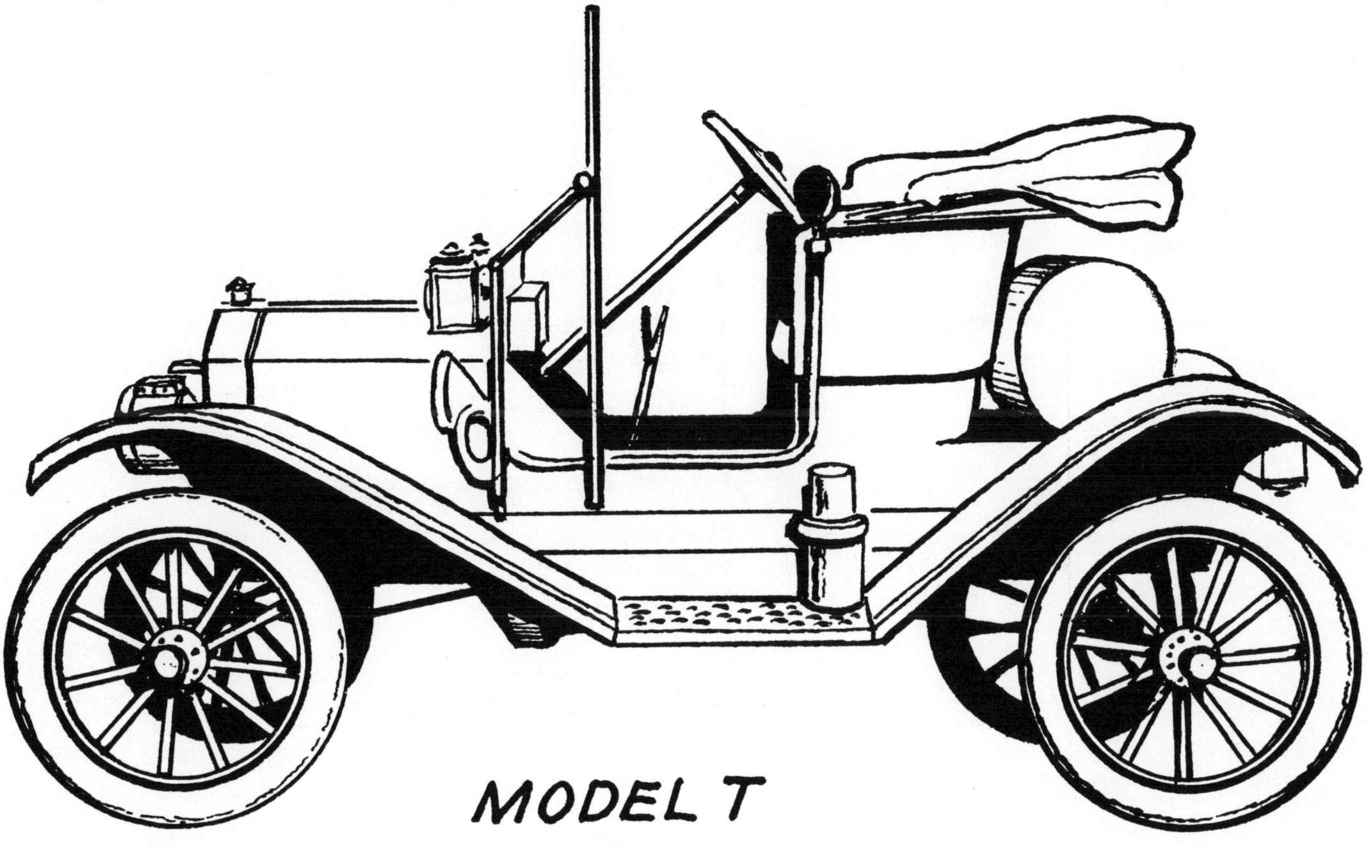

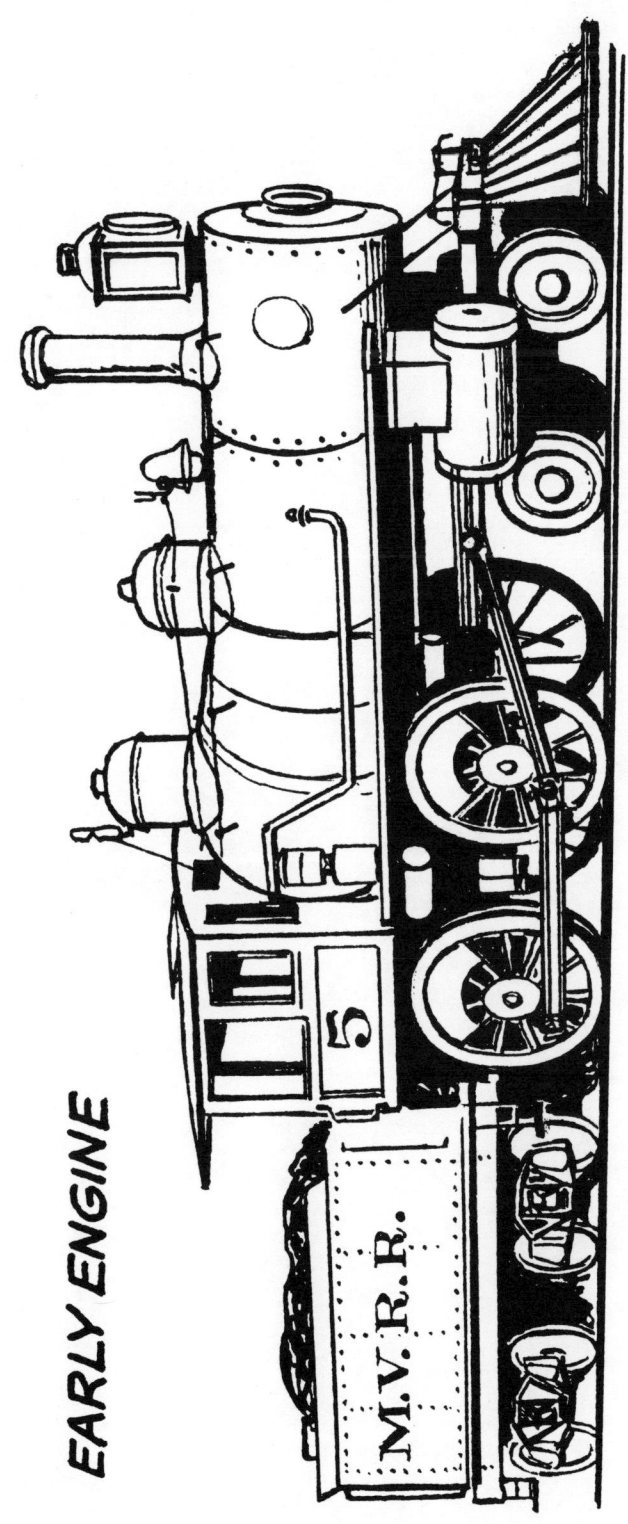

EARLY ENGINE

FARM UNIT

The Farm

POEM I went to the farm and what did I see?
A brown cow and her calf looking at me.

I saw a hen laying eggs in her nest.
A rooster strutting and crowing his best.

I saw a horse in the barn eating hay.
And ducks on the pond enjoying the day.

Last of all I saw the pigs in their pen,
Eating so much they were not very thin.

ART AND CRAFT

Sequence exercise: Read the following paragraphs about the farmer's garden: (children may wish to pantomime the story as you read it). After reading the story, color the pictures which accompany the story, cut out, then arrange in the correct sequence.

Farmer Brown plants seeds in his garden. He plants carrots, lettuce and beans. When the vegetables are ripe, he pulls them out of the ground and off the vines. He loads them into his truck and takes them to the grocery store where he sells them.

Our mother buys these good foods at the store and brings them home. She washes them, cooks them and serves them to us.

"Yum, yum," we say, "these are good!"

Paper garden: Color the bottom of a styrofoam meat tray brown. Let the children cut vegetables from construction paper. Glue to pipe cleaners or toothpicks and stick into tray in rows.

Farm picture: Provide children with a sheet on which has been drawn a barn, a chicken coop, a pond and a fence (see the attached illustration).

Children can color the pictures their appropriate colors and cut them out. On a large sheet of newsprint, glue the barn in place, leaving the door open. Ask the children to draw a picture of an animal that lives in the barn. Next paste the fence near the barn. Ask the children to draw a picture of an animal that they might see in the pasture. Let the children paste the chicken coop onto the newsprint. Encourage the children to draw the hen family around the coop. Paste the pond in place and suggest the children draw a bird which likes to swim in the pond. The children can be encouraged to finish their picture by drawing other things that they might see on the farm.

ACTION POEM

Farm Animals
(response)

Listen to the riddle and you can name
A farm animal when you play this game.

At night my home's a stable . . . it keeps
  out the rain.
My baby is a colt. I eat lots of grass
  and grain. (horse)

I live in a coop and have two legs.
I have feathers. You eat my eggs. (chicken)

I live on a farm. I have four feet.
My baby is a calf. I provide milk and
  meat. (cow)

I help the farmers by catching mice.
I have fur. He treats me nice. (cat)

I stay in a fold at night on the farm.
My coat will keep you very warm. (sheep)

I help the farmer bring in the cows.
Sometimes he takes me into his house.
  (dog)

On the farm I stay in a pen.
My meat gives you sausage and bacon.
  (pig)

Jobs on the Farm
(response)

At the farm there is always work to do.
What am I doing? I'll give you a clue.

If you can guess what I'm doing, do tell.
But please, please speak softly and do
  not yell.

I'm getting small things to put in
  the ground.
I do it quietly and don't make a sound.
  (planting)

A few months later I'm picking things up.
Some will be to sell. Some will be to sup.
  (harvesting)

One thing to do before I go to school.
I'll need a bucket and I'll need a stool.
  (milking)

I'll need a large basket for this next job.
When these animals see me heads will bob.
  (collecting eggs)

There's just one more thing that has
  to be done.
It'll keep in the cows; we won't lose
  a one. (close gate or repair fence)

MUSIC

What Can You Do at the Farm?

(Sing to tune of —
"Oh, Be Careful Little Hands What you do.")

Oh, what can you do at the farm?
Oh, what can you do at the farm?
Say "Moo" to the cow.
He will show you how.
That's what you can do at the farm!

Oh, what can you do at the farm?
Oh, what can you do at the farm?
Watch out for the goat!
For he might eat your coat.
That's what you can do at the farm!

Oh, what can you do at the farm?
Oh, what can you do at the farm?
Plant a few little seeds.
And help to pull the weeds.
That's what you can do at the farm!

Oh, what can you do at the farm?
Oh, what can you do at the farm?
Gather eggs each day.
And feed the horses hay.
That's what you do at the farm!

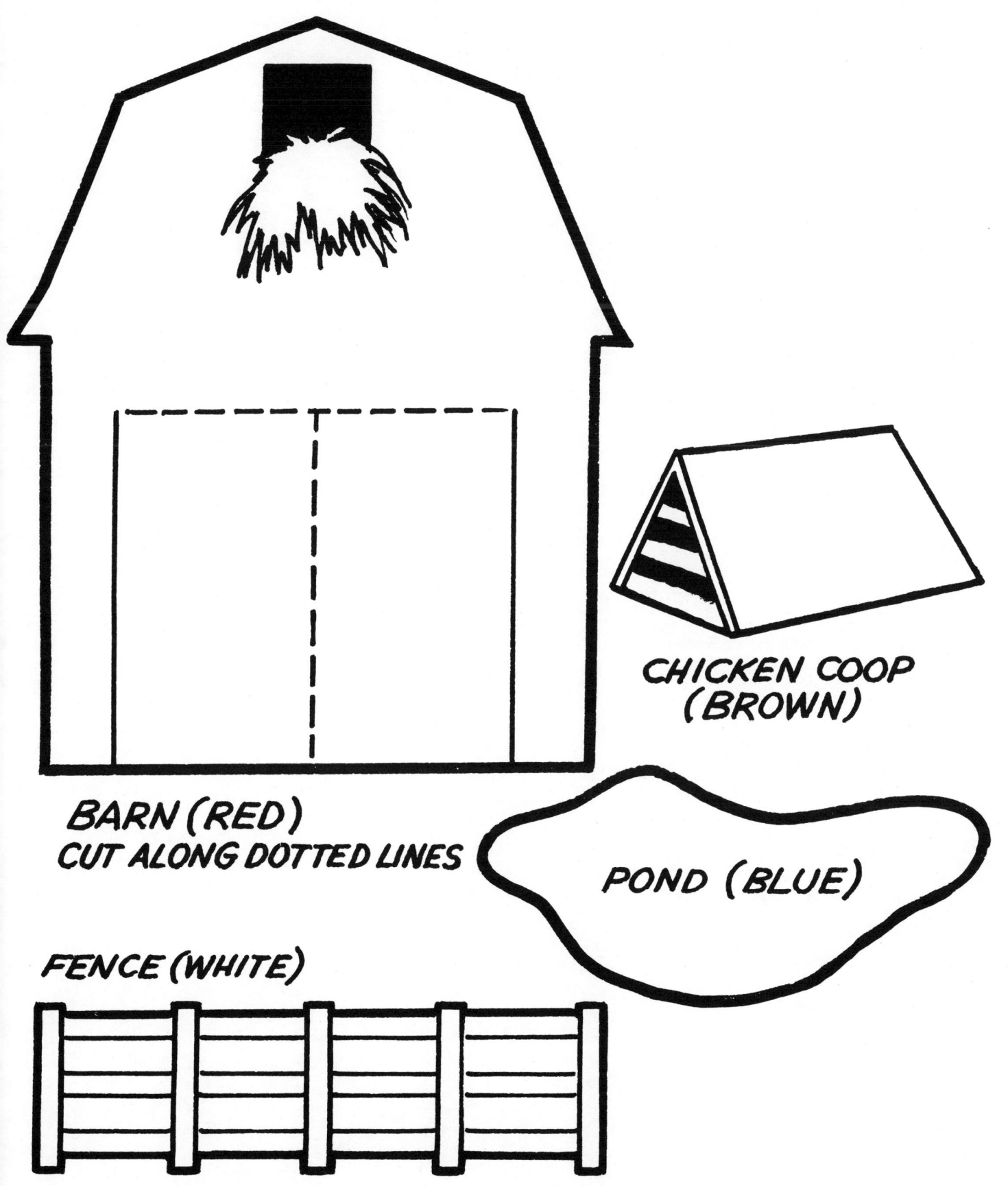

STORY A Day at the Farm

"Good morning, Gary," said Aunt Gretchen. "Are you ready for breakfast?"

Gary had ridden all yesterday to get to the farm. He was going to spend a week with his Uncle George and Aunt Gretchen. Now the first morning had finally arrived and he was ready to help his uncle with the chores.

"You had better eat a good breakfast so you won't get hungry today," said Uncle George.

"How would you like some nice fresh eggs?" asked Aunt Gretchen. "These came from the chickens on the farm and the sausage is some that Uncle George made from one of the pigs. Did you know sausage was made from pigs?"

"No," said Gary. He turned to his uncle. "What does a farmer do all day?"

"I always say 'Good morning' to the animals, then I start working. You come with me today and you can see for yourself. Maybe by the end of the day you'll be ready to be a farmer. Let's go check G.G. first."

Gary was glad his uncle suggested that. "I remember G.G. from last summer. She is the pretty brown horse that I rode after the chores were finished."

They gave G.G. some fresh oats and water, then went to feed the chickens. They were waiting at the chicken coop. Gary threw some feed to them and it wasn't long before the chickens knew they had a new friend. While the chickens ate, Uncle George showed Gary how to check for eggs. They went up and down the rows of nests. That morning they found six fresh eggs, just enough for everyone to have two for breakfast tomorrow morning.

"Can I see the cows next?" asked Gary.

"I milked before breakfast. You can help me put them in the pasture," said Uncle George.

Gary held the gate to the pasture open until all the cattle went through. He closed the gate so that the cows wouldn't get out. He stood on the fence and watched the cows graze.

"Do you want to sit on the tractor while I plow," asked Uncle George.

"This is fun," said Gary as he and his uncle rode up and down the rows on the tractor.

"This is where the wheat will soon be planted," Uncle George explained.

All day Gary helped Uncle George. They fed the pigs and sheep. They pulled weeds from the garden and even picked some fresh vegetables for supper.

At the end of a long day Gary knew that farmers work hard, even if they don't go to the office everyday.

SUPPLEMENTARY IDEAS

Children should have the experience of planting a seed and watching it grow. Stress the importance of soil, sun and water.

Pantomime: feeding chickens, milking cows, gathering eggs, sowing seed and gathering crops.

ADDITIONAL IDEAS
(for teacher use)

SEASHORE UNIT

Seashore

POEM   Let's go to the beach and look for
              some shells.
           We'll look for some limpets, coral and snails.

           And after we've had our shell-hunting fun.
           We'll play near the water and then we'll run.

           We should build a castle with a fine moat.
           In it we could place a tiny sail boat.

ARTS AND CRAFTS

Beach Scene: Using the top of an egg carton, color the bottom half blue for water. Paste on small shells and pieces of driftwood. Draw and color fish, clouds, etc., to complete the scene. A beach scene can also be made in a tissue box. Cut out center, leaving about ½ inch border. Glue cornmeal onto one long side for sand. Add shells. Color in the rest of your scene. A third way to make a beach scene is to fill a baby jar with sand. Arrange pebbles, shells, twigs on top and put lid on. Lid may be sprayed gold. Macaroni can be used for shells. (That is shells made of pasta like macaroni.)

Starfish: Draw a starfish on blue paper. Apply glue and sprinkle on cornmeal. Let dry and remove excess meal. Starfish may also be cut from sandpaper.

Plaque: attach shells to a cedar shingle. (Paint shells with Elmer's Glue.) Shingles can be collected from construction sites. If shells are not avilable, use polished stones or dried flowers or weeds.

Flower arrangements: Put play-dough or florist clay in large shell. Arrange dried flowers in clay. Makes a lovely gift.

Five Little Fishes

FINGERPLAY   Five little fishes
                   Swimming in the bay.
                   The first little fish
                   Turned and swam away.

                   Four little fishes
                   Swimming all around.
                   Two left the others
                   Without 'ere a sound.

Two little fishes
Nibbling on their lunch.
One swam away to
Join another bunch.

The last little fish
Didn't want to roam.
So he decided
To swim slowly home.

MUSIC

Let's go to the Beach
(tune — "A Hunting We Will Go")

Let's go to the beach
To swim and play and run.
Building castles in the sand
Is ever so much fun.

We'll fix a picnic lunch.
And eat it when we like.
And when we all are nice and full
We'll take a nature hike.

Be sure to wear your suit
And bring along your float.
We'll ride so far out in the surf
Pretending it's a boat.

We'll find some pretty shells
And throw the gulls some bread.
Put on a lot of suntan oil
So that we don't turn red.

We'll never want to leave.
Such fun this all has been.
But we'll come back another day.
And do it all again!

STORY

The Treasure Hunt

"We're going on a treasure hunt today boys and girls," said Mrs. Johnson.

The boys and girls in the kindergarten class jumped up and down with excitement.

"Where's the treasure hidden?" asked Johnny.

"On the beach," said Mrs. Johnson. "Let me show you where it's located."

She unfolded a yellowed piece of paper about the size of a newspaper and tacked it on the bulletin board. The children gathered around her as she began explaining the map.

"This is a map of the area where the treasure is hidden," she began, "If you look carefully you will find clues."

The room buzzed with excitement as the children examined the map.

"This is a sand dune," said Janie.

"Here's the picnic tables," said Jeff pointing to the spot on the map where the tables were drawn.

"Is the 'X' the place where the treasure is hidden?" asked Mark.

"That's right!" said their teacher. "The treasure is hidden there. After everyone has made a copy of the treasure map, we'll drive to the beach and see who can find the treasure."

After the children drew their map, they boarded the bus that was to take them to the beach.

"Everyone will line up outside the bus," said Mrs. Johnson when they arrived at the beach. "When I say go, you follow your map and see if you can locate the treasure."

What fun the children had looking for the treasure.

"I've found it," shouted Jeffery a few minutes later. All the children ran to the spot where Jeffrey stood. Underneath a weather-beaten log was a treasure chest.

"Open it! Open it!" yelled the children.

Jeffrey pulled the chest out, lifted the rusty latch and opened the lid.

"Oh!" sighed the children. Inside the chest where tiny objects wrapped in gold paper.

"They look like gold pieces," said Tommy.

"Many years ago when pirates ruled the oceans, they often hid their money chests in inlets along the bay," said their teacher.

Each of the children took a surprise from the chest and opened it. Wrapped inside the shiny gold paper was candy.

"We'll eat the candy after we have your picnic lunch," said Mrs. Johnson.

What a nice way to end a treasure hunt!

(After the story let the children make a treasure chest. One method is to glue toothpicks to a toothpick box. Paint or spray box. Add some "treasures". You may also cover any small box with brown construction paper. Use a felt pen to draw lines on paper to give the appearance of wood. Paper handles can be glued to ends.)

SUPPLEMENTARY IDEAS

Visit the beach if possible. Let the children collect shells, build a sandcastle and feed the seagulls.

Supplier of shells:
   SEVEN SEAS
   Flour Bluff Station
   Corpus Christi, Texas 78418

ADDITIONAL IDEAS
(for teachers use)

MISCELLANEOUS

Colors

POEMS Blue is the color we see in the sky.
Black is the color of a tiny fly.

Brown is the color of a mountain bear.
Yellow's the color of a juicy pear.

Orange is the color of oranges we eat.
Green is the color of grass on my street.

Purple's the color we see on some grapes.
Red is the color of bullfighters' capes.

The Clever Pirates

Clever pirates are we.
We live way out at sea.
When the ships come around
We will take all they've found.
And that's why we're rich you see.

ARTS AND CRAFTS

Yarn numbers: Let the children paste yarn to numbers which have been printed on lightweight cardboard or construction paper. (this may also be used with letters) In place of yarn, the children could roll play dough into thin strips and place over the numbers.

Place mats: Children can make mats to go with units of study or the seasons. Use construction paper with cut-outs pasted on; wax paper with magic markers or decorated paper towels.

Fabric pictures: Attach dried flowers to fabric samples. Frame can be cut from construction paper and glued onto the fabric edges. Fabric samples can be obtained from discarded samples at decorator shops.

Car hats: Draw an outline of a car (or any vehicle) on the fold of a piece of construction paper. The child can cut out and tape the ends together for a hat.

Duck on a pond: Have the children cut out a duck shape (one may be provided) from construction paper. An oblong pond can be cut from blue paper. Slit the center of the pond so the duck can be inserted and moved back and forth across the pond.

Clothespin animal: Using a wooden clothespin and scraps of construction paper, children can use their imagination to make animal figures.

Turtle: Glue or tape a cardboard (or paper) circle to the back of a spoon (wooden or plastic). Yarn can be looped for legs and glued to circle.

FINGERPLAY

Five Little Pirates

Five little pirates heard the gun roar.
One raised his black flag, then there were four.
Four little pirates sailing on the sea.
One tumbled overboard, then there were three.
Three little pirates on the ocean blue,
One swam away, then there were two.
Two little pirates fighting in the sun,
One used a sword, then there was one.
One little pirate liked to have fun,
He found a treasure chest, then were were none.

STORY

Spotted Puppy Finds his Home

One sunny day little Spotted Puppy was playing in the yard when he decided to take a walk around his neighborhood to see what he could see.

Spotted Puppy sniffed the smells of Fall. He tiptoed through the orange, yellow, and brown leaves that had fallen from the trees and heard the crunch they made when he walked over them.

Before to long Spotted Puppy began to get hungry. When he turned to go home, he discovered he was lost. He sat down and began to cry.

"What's the matter, Spotted Puppy?" chirped Red Bird from her nest in the tree.

"I'm lost," said Spotted Puppy. "I want to go home."

"You can stay with me in my home," offered Red Bird.

"Thank you, Red Bird," said Spotted Puppy, "but I'm too big to fit in your nest."

"There's another home down by the pond," said Red Bird. "Maybe it's your home."

Spotted Puppy walked to the pond. "Have you seen my home?" he asked Tommie Turtle who was sun bathing along the grassy bank of the pond.

"No," said Tommie Turtle. "You could stay with me but I don't have room." Tommie Turtle patted his shell.

Spotted Puppy was getting very tired and hungry so he said goodbye to Tommie Turtle and walked on down the path. Soon he came upon a hole in the ground. "Maybe this is my home" Spotted Puppy said and stuck his nose inside to look around. But to Spotted Puppy's surprise there was a mother rabbit and four baby bunnies curled up and sound asleep.

By now Spotted Puppy was so hungry that he began to sniff around for some dinner. He smelled something sweet and followed the smell until he was upon a beehive. Now Spotted Puppy did not know that this was the home of the Bee family. All he knew was that he was hungry. When he stuck his paw into the beehive to get some of the sweet honey, Mother Bee stung him.

"Ouch," cried Spotted Puppy. Off he ran down the path. Suddenly he saw someone very familiar.

"Where have you been?" called Mother Dog. "I've been looking for you everywhere."

"I've been lost," answered Spotted Puppy. "I'm so glad to be back home."

Spotted Puppy ran to the dish of food which sat outside his doghouse. "There's no place like home," he said and gobbled up his dinner.

Note: This story is used effectively as a flannel board story.

Turtles: Cut two bodies from wallpaper samples (some samples are very appropriate colors for turtles). Cut the head on the fold and glue together. Glue the body together at feet only. Insert the head into body cavity and it will wiggle. Head should not be glued inside the body.

Tammie's Gift of Love

Tammie watched her older sister wrap a gift. Her sister, Ann, had painted a beautiful picture for a Mother's Day gift for their mother.

"I wish I could paint a pretty picture for Mother," said Tammie.

"What are you going to give Mother?" asked Ann.

"I don't know," said Tammie.

The next two days Tammie thought and thought about what she could give her mother for Mother's Day. She was too small to make something like Ann had made. But she wanted to show her mother how much she loved her.

On Mother's Day, Tammie awakened early. She still hadn't decided what gift to give her mother. She was very sad. She leaned on her window sill and looked outside.

"I want to show Mother that I love her," she thought.

As she was thinking, Tammie smelled a sweet fragrance. Near her window beautiful roses were blooming. Suddenly Tammie smiled happily. She ran from her room and out the front door. She clipped a beautiful yellow rose bud from the bush and took it inside.

In the kitchen, she found a bud vase and placed the rose inside. Tammie ran excitedly to her mother's room. Her mother opened her eyes and smiled at her little daughter.

"Happy Mother's Day," said Tammie. "I love you."

"Oh, how beautiful," said her mother. "I shall enjoy the sweet smell of this flower for days. What a lovely gift."

Tammie smiled. She was pleased that she made her mother so happy.

SUPPLEMENTARY IDEAS

Provide a box of sand (small). Let the children draw numbers with their fingers. This is excellent for the sense of touch.

Numbers game: Supply six green cards with numbers printed on the back and six orange cards with identical numbers. Turn the green cards number side down on a table Leave the orange cards number side up. A child chooses one green card. He tries to match the number on this card to the card with the same number on the orange card. Children take turns drawing green cards.

Math readiness: Clip plastic curtain rings in a chain. Use this to illustrate greater than or less than; above and below, etc.

Shapes: Have a small triangle, a large triangle and a large circle draw on a sheet. Provide each child with a sheet. Instruct the class to color the small triangle red; the circle blue; the large triangle yellow. Use other shapes and colors. This is good to test the child early in the year to see if he knows basic shapes and colors.

Body numbers: Children can make numbers by laying on the floor in various positions. See the examples below.

Printing on vinyl overlays: The teacher prints a letter or number she wants the child to practice printing, on a sheet of paper.

Using a vinyl sheet (cut from wallpaper sample books where they are used to separate the flocked paper) the child traces the number with a crayon. These can be wiped clean and used over and over. After the child has mastered the number or letter, he may try to print it by himself on paper.

Sound recognition: To reinforce sound recognition, ask each child a question he can answer using a word that starts with the letter the class is studying.

Tying shoes: Make a bunny ear with one lace, then another ear with the other lace. Tie his ears together and make a head. The ends of the laces are the bunny's whiskers.

Communication match up: Have pictures of the following types of communication. Read a question about each type and let the children match to the correct picture.
1. Telephone
2. Satellite
3. Television
4. Telegraph
5. Radio
6. Newspaper
7. Magazines and Books

Questions:
1. What do we listen to while traveling in a car?
2. What is the quickest way of speaking to grandmother who lives in another city.?
3. How can we hear and see what is happening in our city and other cities?
4. Where can we read a story about a famous person?
5. How can we hear of news from across the world while it is happening?
6. How can we send a speedy message to a friend?
7. How is news delivered to our doorstep everyday?

ADDITIONAL IDEAS
(for teacher use)